First Workshop on Advances in Language and Vision Research 2020

Online
9 July 2020

ISBN: 978-1-7138-1375-0

Printed from e-media with permission by:

Curran Associates, Inc.
57 Morehouse Lane
Red Hook, NY 12571

CURRAN ASSOCIATES INC.
proceedings
.com

Some format issues inherent in the e-media version may also appear in this print version.

Association for Computational Linguistics
209 N. Eighth Street
Stroudsburg, Pennsylvania 18360

Phone: 1-570-476-8006
Fax: 1-570-476-0860

acl@aclweb.org

Additional copies of this publication are available from:

Curran Associates, Inc.
57 Morehouse Lane
Red Hook, NY 12571 USA
Phone: 845-758-0400
Fax: 845-758-2633
Email: curran@proceedings.com
Web: www.proceedings.com

ACL 2020

Advances in Language and Vision Research

Proceedings of the First Workshop

July 9, 2020

Introduction

Language and vision research has attracted great attention from both natural language processing (NLP) and computer vision (CV) researchers. Gradually, this area is shifting from passive perception, templated language, and synthetic imagery or environments to active perception, natural language, and photo-realistic simulation or real world deployment. Thus far, few workshops on language and vision research have been organized by groups from the NLP community. We organize the first workshop on Advances in Language and Vision Research (ALVR) in order to promote the frontier of language and vision research and to bring interested researchers together to discuss how to best tackle and solve real-world problems in this area.

Organizers:

Xin Wang, UC Santa Barbara
Jesse Thomason, University of Washington
Ronghang Hu, UC Berkeley
Xinlei Chen, Facebook AI Research
Peter Anderson, Georgia Tech
Qi Wu, Adelaide University
Asli Celikyilmaz, Microsoft Research
Jason Baldridge, Google Research
William Yang Wang, UC Santa Barbara

Program Committee:

Jacob Andreas, MIT
Angel Chang, Simon Fraser Univeristy
Devendra Chaplot, CMU
Abhishek Das, Georgia Tech
Daniel Fried, UC Berkeley
Zhe Gan, Microsoft
Christopher Kanan, Rochester Institute of Technology
Jiasen Lu, Georgia Tech
Ray Mooney, University of Texas, Austin
Khanh Nguyen, University of Maryland
Aishwarya Padmakumar, University of Texas, Austin
Hamid Palangi, Microsoft Research
Alessandro Suglia, Heriot-Watt University
Vikas Raunak, CMU
Volkan Cirik, CMU
Parminder Bhatia, Amazon
Khyathi Raghavi Chandu, CMU
Asma Ben Abacha, NIH/NLM
Thoudam Doren Singh, National Institute of Technology, Silchar, India
Dhivya Chinnappa, Thomson Reuters
Shailza Jolly, TU Kaiserslautern
Alok Singh, National Institute of Technology, Silchar, India
Mohamed Elhoseiny, KAUST
Marimuthu Kalimuthu, Saarland University
Simon Dobnik, University of Gothenburg
Shruti Palaskar, CMU

Invited Speaker:

Yoav Artzi, Cornell
Joyce Chai, University of Michigan
JJ (Jingjing) Liu, Microsoft
Louis-Philippe Morency, CMU
Mark Riedl, Georgia Tech
Lucia Specia, Imperial College London
Zhou Yu, UC Davis

Table of Contents

Workshop Program

Workshop schedule details: https://alvr-workshop.github.io

The workshop also holds the first Video-guided Machine Translation (VMT) challenge and the REVERIE challenge. The VMT challenge aims to benchmark progress towards models that translate source language sentence into the target language with video information as the additional spatiotemporal context. The challenge is based on the recently released large-scale multilingual video description dataset, VATEX. The VATEX dataset contains over 41,250 videos and 825,000 high-quality captions in both English and Chinese, half of which are English-Chinese translation pairs. The REVERIE challenge requires an intelligent agent to correctly localize a remote target object (cannot be observed at the starting location) specified by a concise high-level natural language instruction, such as "bring me the blue cushion from the sofa in the living room". Since the target object is in a different room from the starting one, the agent needs first to navigate to the goal location. When the agent determines to stop, it should select one object from a list of candidates provided by the simulator. The agent can attempt to localize the target at any step, which is totally up to algorithm design. But the agent is only allowed to output once in each episode, which means the agent only can guess the answer once in a single run.

Archival track papers presented at the workshop:

Extending ImageNet to Arabic using Arabic WordNet
Abdulkareem Alsudais

Toward General Scene Graph: Integration of Visual Semantic Knowledge with Entity Synset Alignment
Woo Suk Choi, Kyoung-Woon On, Yu-Jung Heo and Byoung-Tak Zhang

Visual Question Generation from Radiology Images
Mourad Sarrouti, Asma Ben Abacha and Dina Demner-Fushman

On the role of effective and referring questions in GuessWhat?!
Mauricio Mazuecos, Alberto Testoni, Raffaella Bernardi and Luciana Benotti

Latent Alignment of Procedural Concepts in Multimodal Recipes
Hossein Rajaby Faghihi, Roshanak Mirzaee, Sudarshan Paliwal and Parisa Kordjamshidi

Extending ImageNet to Arabic using Arabic WordNet

Abdulkareem Alsudais
College of Computer Engineering and Sciences, Prince Sattam bin Abdulaziz University
Al-Kharj, Saudi Arabia
A.Alsudais@psau.edu.sa

Abstract

ImageNet has millions of images that are labeled with English WordNet synsets. This paper investigates the extension of ImageNet to Arabic using Arabic WordNet. The objective is to discover if Arabic synsets can be found for synsets used in ImageNet. The primary finding is the identification of Arabic synsets for 1,219 of the 21,841 synsets used in ImageNet, which represents 1.1 million images. By leveraging the parent-child structure of synsets in ImageNet, this dataset is extended to 10,462 synsets (and 7.1 million images) that have an Arabic label, which is either a match or a direct hypernym, and to 17,438 synsets (and 11 million images) when a hypernym of a hypernym is included. When all hypernyms for a node are considered, an Arabic synset is found for all but four synsets. This represents the major contribution of this work: a dataset of images that have Arabic labels for 99.9% of the images in ImageNet.

1 Introduction

ImageNet is a dataset comprised of 14 million images (Deng et al., 2009; Russakovsky et al., 2015). Each image in the dataset is labeled with a WordNet (Miller, 1995) synset representing the identifying object in the image. The fall 2011 release of the dataset has a total of 21,841 unique synsets that are used to label images. The dataset is organized by dividing these synsets into several major subtrees. Moreover, ImageNet is structured in a way that maintains the semantic hierarchical structure of synsets in WordNet, where each image is also linked to branches of hypernyms (Figure 1). ImageNet is one major reason for recent advances in computer vision research and deep learning (Cetinic et al., 2018; Stock and Cisse, 2018; Kornblith et al., 2019).

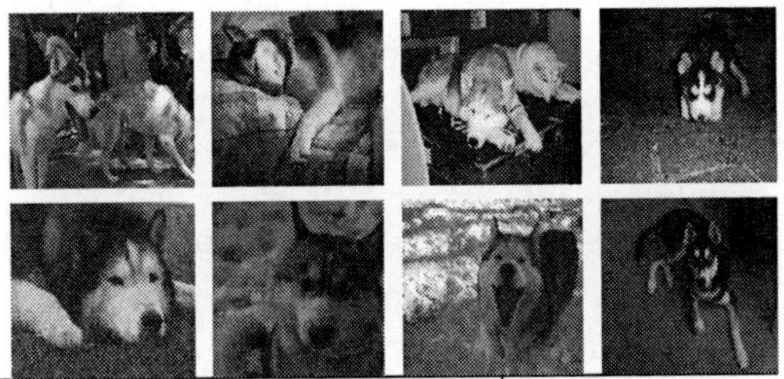

Synset in ImageNet	Arabic Synset from AWN
0. Siberian husky	*not available*
1. Sled dog: Direct hypernym for "siberian husky".	*not available*
2. Working dog: Hypernym for "sled dog".	كلب عامل، كلب الشغل
3. Dog: Hypernym for "working dog".	كلب

Figure 1: Images in ImageNet for the synset "Siberian husky". Although an Arabic synset from AWN is not available for the synset or its direct hypernym, one is available for the hypernym of the hypernym.

While computer vision research has seen significant progress in recent years, the focus has been on English. Limited work exists to extend research to other languages, including Arabic. This lack of research may present challenges to scientists, researchers, and practitioners who seek to address problems related to computer vision in Arabic. Furthermore, the unavailability of a large dataset of images labeled in Arabic may prevent the development of solutions that address challenging tasks, such as visual question answering and image classification in Arabic. Therefore, a large dataset of images labeled with Arabic has the potential to progress research in Arabic computer vision. Moreover, scholars studying Arabic natural language processing often develop methods specifically designed for Arabic. Thus, it is possible that similarly unique methods are needed for Arabic computer vision.

Proceedings of the First Workshop on Advances in Language and Vision Research, pages 1–6

The primary objective of this paper is to investigate the effectiveness of extending ImageNet to Arabic using Arabic WordNet (AWN) by searching in AWN for all the synsets used in ImageNet. AWN was originally developed in 2006 (Black et al., 2006). Since then, several authors have attempted to extend it by improving its coverage or quality (Alkhalifa and Rodríguez, 2009; Abouenour et al., 2013; Bond and Foster, 2013; Regragui et al., 2016; Batita et al., 2019). The possibility of using AWN to extend ImageNet has been experimented with in one paper (Alsudais, 2019). In the paper, the author tested using AWN to find Arabic synsets for a small sample of 100 images from ImageNet and indicated that Arabic synsets were found for only six synsets. However, the author did not attempt to discover if Arabic synsets were available for hypernyms of these synsets. This paper attempts to overcome the problems of limited availability for direct matches by also searching branches of hypernyms in AWN. In summary, this paper makes three major contributions:

- It investigates the possibility of extending ImageNet to Arabic using the Arabic WordNet (AWN).
- It adds to the limited work in computer vision research in Arabic.
- It generates a new, large dataset of images with Arabic labels. This dataset includes at least one label for all but four of the 21,841 synsets used in ImageNet.

ImageNet has been used to solve tasks in the intersection of language and vision research (Zhou et al., 2018; Chen et al., 2019; Davis et al., 2019; Vempala and Preot, 2019). For Arabic computer vision, limited related work currently exists. Several authors have worked on the generation of Arabic captions for images (Jindal, 2018; Al-muzaini et al., 2018). In another paper, a new dataset related to Arabic computer vision was built. The authors constructed a dataset of 3,000 clips that they classified with emotional labels such as "happy", "sad", or "angry" (Shaqra et al., 2019). The authors argued that emotional facial expressions may be different depending on the cultural context. In other papers, attempts to connect ImageNet to external resources were made by linking the synsets in ImageNet to items in Wikidata (Nielsen, 2018) and by extending a sample of images in ImageNet to German using human subjects, which resulted in a dataset of 1,305,602 images (Roller and Schulte, 2013). In the only other closely related paper, the author investigated the possibility of generating Arabic labels for images in ImageNet using an online translator (Alsudais, 2019). In the paper, the author targeted a sample of 1,895 images from ImageNet and used an online translator to generate Arabic labels for the synsets. A human judge then evaluated the accuracy of the translations. The results indicated that the translations were accurate for 65% of the images, which represented 1,643 unique synsets and 1,910,935 images. This suggests that solely using a translator to translate labels of images in ImageNet may not produce highly accurate results.

2 Extending ImageNet to Arabic using Arabic WordNet

In ImageNet, each synset has a name and an ID. To begin exploring the possibility of finding Arabic synsets and labels for images in ImageNet using AWN, all the synsets' IDs are retrieved from ImageNet. There are several releases for ImageNet. In this paper, the fall 2011 release is used. This release includes 21,841 unique WordNet synsets, and each is linked to one or many images. For example, the synset ID "n07873807" includes 1,296 images of "pizza". There are also 1,186 images for "dish", the direct hypernym for "pizza". Moreover, all the images labeled with "pizza" can also be labeled with "dish". Since "dish" is a hypernym for several other synsets used in ImageNet, such as "sushi" and "curry", the number of images for "dish" extends to all images with a synset that is a hyponym (child) for "dish".

ImageNet's data are downloaded directly from ImageNet's website[1]. ImageNet provides the URLs of the images. These URLs are viewed in order to access the images. Due to ongoing developments related to the removal of problematic images present in the "person" subtree, ImageNet no longer provides a method to download the full dataset directly (Yang et al., 2020). The dataset has a total of 14,197,122 images. Each synset has an average of 944 images directly assigned to the synset. The minimum number of images is 1 image, and the maximum is 2,382 images for a synset.

[1] http://www.image-net.org/download.php

2.1 Direct Arabic Synsets for Synsets in ImageNet

The first step is to investigate if Arabic synsets are available for each of the 21,841 synsets used in ImageNet. To complete this, all the synsets IDs are processed. For each synset, AWN is searched to find a direct match. There are several versions of AWN and several methods to access it currently exist. To gain additional knowledge on WordNet and AWN, and to determine a reliable method to access it, the online interfaces for both the Open Multilingual WordNet (OMW)[2] (Bond and Paik, 2012) and the Princeton WordNet[3] (Princeton University, 2010) are tested. Additionally, the WordNet interface in the python library NLTK[4] is tested. The interface includes the OMW, which has AWN (Black et al., 2006; Abouenour et al., 2013). This version of AWN has 9,916 Arabic synsets, which is less than the number of synsets used in ImageNet. This is the first indicator that it may not be possible to find direct matches for all synsets. Still, it is not clear if it is possible for a synset in ImageNet to be directly linked to several synsets in AWN. Based on this experimental phase, the NLTK interface is selected to access Arabic synsets in AWN. ImageNet uses WordNet 3.0, which has synsets IDs that are different than one used in WordNet 3.1. Therefore, the results in this paper are necessarily achieved by using WordNet 3.0.

2.2 Arabic Synsets for Hypernyms

Since ImageNet structures synsets based on the semantic structure of synsets in WordNet, a synset in ImageNet is essentially a node that is connected to a branch or several branches of hypernyms. The objective of this step is to discover if an Arabic synset in AWN is available for the list of hypernyms linked to a synset. To accomplish this, the parent-child (or hypernym-hyponym) pairs in ImageNet are downloaded from a webpage in ImageNet's website[5]. Algorithm 1 includes details of the steps followed in order to find direct matches as well as Arabic hypernyms for synsets. The algorithm relies on the use of a recursive function that looks for an Arabic synset for all the hypernyms connected to the synset at all levels. The stopping condition for this recursive function is when all possible hypernyms are processed.

Algorithm 1: Finding direct AWN synsets for ImageNet's synsets as well as AWN synsets for all the hypernyms linked to ImageNet's synsets.

Input: list of all synsets in ImageNet. "Synset" below refers to the synset from ImageNet.

Output: 1) Direct_AWN: list of Arabic synsets from AWN that are directly linked to a synset in ImageNet, and 2) Hyper_AWN: a list of Arabic synsets from AWN that are linked to a hypernym of a synset in ImageNet.

```
For synset in ImageNet:
  If find_in_AWN (synset) is True then
    Direct_AWN.add (synset, AWN_synset)
  Find_Hypers (synset, synset, 1)
func Find_Hypers (synset, hyper_synset, level):
  Hypers=get_hypers (hyper_synset)
  If length (Hypers) == 0:
    Stop #no more hypernyms to process
  For hyper_synset in Hypers:
    If find_in_AWN (hyper_synset) is True then
      Hyper_AWN.add (synset,
                hyper_ AWN_synset, level)
    Find_Hypers (synset, hyper_synset, level+1)
```

To complete this process, all hypernyms of a synset are retrieved. In most cases, a synset that is a leaf node has one or two direct hypernyms. Each hypernym is searched for in AWN in order to discover if an Arabic synset for the hypernym exist in AWN. If one is found, it is added to the set of Arabic synsets for the primary synset. The level of the hypernym is also saved. For example, since an Arabic synset is available for the synset "dish", which happens to be a hypernym for "pizza", the Arabic synset for "dish" is saved for the "pizza" synset. Additionally, the number "one" is saved because "dish" is a direct hypernym for "pizza". Similarity, the number "two" is saved for "nutriment", which is the hypernym for "dish". If a synset has two direct hypernyms, they are both saved as appearing in level one. Hypernyms are only saved when an Arabic synset is found.

This step results in a dataset of all AWN synsets in ImageNet, as well as the Arabic synsets available at each level of their hypernyms. Since it is possible for a synset to have two hypernyms, the objective of searching hypernyms is to indicate if *any* Arabic synsets exist for *any* of the hypernyms. It is unclear if using hypernyms to label images in Arabic will produce images with acceptable and meaningful labels. Future work should investigate the quality of generated Arabic sysnets.

[2] http://compling.hss.ntu.edu.sg/omw/

[3] http://wordnet-rdf.princeton.edu/

[4] http://www.nltk.org/howto/wordnet.html

[5] http://www.image-net.org/archive/wordnet.is_a.txt

3 Results

3.1 Direct Arabic Synsets

Images	ImageNet Synset	AWN Synset
	n00017222: plant.n.02	حياة_نباتِيّة، غرْسة، نبات
	n03405725: furniture.n.01	أثاث، قِطْعة_أثاث
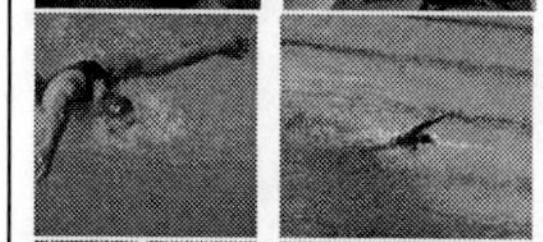	n00442115: swimming.n.01	سِباحة، عوْم
	n13100156: poisonous_plant.n.01	نبات_سامّ

Table 1: Examples of images from ImageNet with their synsets and Arabic synsets, as found in AWN.

Direct matches were found for 1,219 of the 21,841 synsets used in ImageNet. Some of these identified synsets are of higher-level categories, while others are of fine-grained ones. Table 1 includes examples of images where an Arabic synset was found in AWN. The table also shows both the English and Arabic synsets. Since each synset is linked to many images, the dataset of 1,219 synsets was extended to 1,150,651 images, which is 8.1% of ImageNet's total number of images. This dataset represents a major contribution of the paper, as it can be used in several tasks related to Arabic computer vision. Since all the labels are of direct matches, the quality of the labels should be high. However, further examination and full evaluations are needed for confirmation.

3.2 Arabic Synsets for Hypernyms

To expand the dataset, hypernyms of synsets used in ImageNet were searched for in AWN. The result of this extension was the identification of Arabic synsets for all but four synsets used in ImageNet. These four synsets include only 1,366 images. This indicates that there are only 1,366 images in ImageNet without Arabic synsets in AWN for the synset or one of its hypernyms in its branch of hypernyms. A detailed summary of the results is presented in Table 2. In the table, "AWN's synsets" refers to the number of Arabic synsets found for a synset in ImageNet at each level. The "AWN's synset + previous" refers to the total number of Arabic synsets identified when the synsets found at level and the previous levels are combined. The "Images in ImageNet" refers to the total number of images found for each Arabic synset at each level.

When only the first and second level hypernyms were considered, the dataset included Arabic synsets for 79.8% of the synsets and 81.2% of the images in ImageNet. This represents a large dataset of 11,533,525 images, all labeled with an Arabic synset that is either the direct match for the synset used in ImageNet, the Arabic synset for the hypernym, or the Arabic synset for the hypernym of a hypernym. Although a synset in this subset (Row #5 in Table 2) was found for 17,438 of the synsets used in ImageNet, many of the identified Arabic synsets were used more than once since the total number of synsets in AWN is only 9,916. It is important to note that as the level of the hypernym increases, the hypernym become more abstract and general. For example, some of the 7th-level hypernyms include "entity", "act", and "event". Therefore, the usability of Arabic synsets at higher levels requires additional investigation.

Level	AWN's Synsets	AWN's Synsets + Previous	Images in ImageNet	Images + Previous
Direct	1,219 (5.58%)	------------------	1,150,651 (8.1%)	------------------
No person subtree	993 (5.22%)		990,189 (7.6%)	
First Hypernym	10,400 (47.6%)	10,462 (47.9%)	7,113,853 (50.1%)	7,177,537 (50.5%)
No person subtree	8,846 (46.5%)	8,890 (46.7%)	6,419,390 (49.3%)	6,469,802 (49.7%)
2nd Hypernym	16,837 (77.0%)	17,438 (79.8%)	11,088,519 (78.1%)	11,533,525 (81.2%)
No person subtree	14,541 (76.5%)	15,064 (79.2%)	10,099,744 (77.6%)	10,508,392 (80.7%)
3rd Hypernym	19,490 (89.2%)	20,267 (93.7%)	12,697,838 (89.4%)	13,266,956 (93.4%)
4th Hypernym	20,671 (94.6%)	21,397 (97.9%)	13,365,182 (94.1%)	13,916,531 (98.0%)
5th Hypernym	20,816 (95.3%)	21,751 (99.5%)	13,483,006 (94.9%)	14,148,669 (99.6%)
6th Hypernym	19,910 (91.1%)	21,830 (99.94%)	12,865,510 (90.6%)	14,195,325 (99.8%)
7th Hypernym	18,191 (83.2%)	21,837 (99.98%)	11,729,718 (82.6%)	14,195,756 (99.9%)

Table 2: Summary of the number of synsets and number of images found.

While this dataset of Arabic synsets for images in ImageNet is likely reliable since it is based on the utilization of previously existing and evaluated datasets, certain characteristic of the Arabic language and naming decisions in AWN suggest that proper evaluation of the dataset's accuracy may be needed. For example, one of the synsets found in AWN was "nurse". Unlike English, Arabic nouns are gendered. Accordingly, in AWN the Arabic synset for "nurse" is "male nurse". Therefore, an automated image classification system that relies on this synset may suggest "male nurse" for images of female nurses.

This "nurse" synset is part of the "person" subtree, which is one of the major subtrees in ImageNet. This subtree includes several synsets that have been criticized for issues such as representation biases and offensive images (Shankar et al., 2017; Mehrabi et al., 2019). During this study, it was observed that images in the "Iraqi" synset were mostly war related. Additional issues were discovered for images in the "Syrian" synset. Recently, some of the scientists behind ImageNet addressed concerns regarding issues in the "person" subtree and indicated that an upgrade of ImageNet will be released with two changes: 1) only up to 158 of the 2,832 synsets in the "person" subtree will be kept, and 2) attention will be given to representation biases in images in the synsets that are not removed (Yang et al., 2020). In anticipation for these updates, Table 2 also includes results obtained when the 2,832 synsets in the "person" subtree were not included. These results suggest only a minor decrease in percentages of synsets found in each level.

4 Conclusion

In this paper, the possibility of extending ImageNet to Arabic is investigated. The following discoveries were made: 1) an Arabic synset in AWN exists for 1,219 of the synsets used in ImageNet, which represents 1,150,651 images, and 2) Arabic synsets in AWN exist for 99.9% of the images in ImageNet when the branches of hypernyms for synsets were considered. To improve the results found, several options are available. One option is to use the Extended Open Multilingual Wordnet (1.2), which enhances Arabic WordNet by utilizing Wiktionary and Unicode Common Locale Data Repository (Bond and Foster, 2013). This automatic extension of AWN increases the total number of unique synsets available in AWN to 14,650 synsets. Using this version of AWN would likely find Arabic synsets for additional images used in ImageNet. Several other directions for future work exist. One important extension is to provide an extensive evaluation of the dataset. Another avenue for further research would involve investigating the availably of Arabic synsets for each of the synsets in ImageNet's 1,000 object classes, as this subset is often used in computer vision research.

References

Lahsen Abouenour, Karim Bouzoubaa, and Paolo Rosso. 2013. On the evaluation and improvement of Arabic WordNet coverage and usability. Language Resources and Evaluation, 47:891–917.

Musa Alkhalifa and Horacio Rodríguez. 2009. Automatically extending NE coverage of Arabic WordNet using Wikipedia. In The 3rd International Conference on Arabic Language Processing CITALA2009., pages 20–36, Rabat, Morocco.

Huda A Al-muzaini, Tasniem N Al-yahya, and Hafida Benhidour. 2018. Automatic Arabic Image Captioning using RNN-LSTM-Based Language Model and CNN. International Journal of Advanced Computer Science and Applications, 9(6):67–73.

Abdulkareem Alsudais. 2019. Image Classification in Arabic: Exploring Direct English to Arabic Translations. IEEE Access, 7:122730–122739.

Mohamed Ali Batita, Rami Ayadi, and Mounir Zrigui. 2019. Reasoning over Arabic WordNet Relations with Neural Tensor Network. Computación y Sistemas, 23(3):935–942.

William Black, Sabri Elkateb, Horacio Rodriguez, Musa Alkhalifa, Piek Vossen, Adam Pease, and Christiane Fellbaum. 2006. Introducing the Arabic WordNet Project. In Proceedings of the third international WordNet conference., pages 295–299.

Francis Bond and Ryan Foster. 2013. Linking and Extending an Open Multilingual Wordnet. In Proceedings of the 51st Annual Meeting of the Association for Computational Linguistics, pages 1352–1362, Sofia, Bulgaria. Association for Computational Linguistics.

Francis Bond and Kyonghee Paik. 2012. A Survey of WordNets and their Licenses. In Proceedings of the 6th Global WordNet Conference (GWC 2012), pages 64–71.

Eva Cetinic, Tomislav Lipic, and Sonja Grgic. 2018. Fine-tuning Convolutional Neural Networks for fine art classification. Expert Systems With Applications, 114:107–118.

Zhenfang Chen, Lin Ma, Wenhan Luo, and Kwan-Yee K.Wong. 2019. Weakly-Supervised Spatio-Temporally Grounding Natural Sentence in Video. In Proceedings of the 57th Annual Meeting of the Association for Computational Linguistics, pages 1884–1894, Florence, Italy, July 28 - August 2, 2019. Association for Computational Linguistics.

Christopher Davis, Luana Bulat, Anita Vero, and Ekaterina Shutova. 2019. Deconstructing multimodality: visual properties and visual context in human semantic processing. In Proceedings of the Eighth Joint Conference on Lexical and Computational Semantics (*SEM), pages 118–124, Minneapolis, June 6–7, 2019. Association for Computational Linguistics.

Jia Deng, Wei Dong, Richard Socher, Li-jia Li, Kai Li, and Li Fei-fei. 2009. ImageNet: A large-scale hierarchical image database. In 2009 IEEE Conference on Computer Vision and Pattern Recognition, pages 248–255, Miami, FL.

Vasu Jindal. 2018. Generating image captions in Arabic using root-word based recurrent neural networks and deep neural networks. In Proceedings of NAACL-HLT 2018: Student Research Workshop, pages 144–151.

Simon Kornblith, Jonathon Shlens, and Quoc V Le. 2019. Do Better ImageNet Models Transfer Better? In Proceedings of the IEEE conference on computer vision and pattern recognition, pages 2661–2671.

Ninareh Mehrabi, Fred Morstatter, Nripsuta Saxena, Kristina Lerman, and Aram Galstyan. 2019. A Survey on Bias and Fairness in Machine Learning. arXiv:1908.09635v2.

George A Miller. 1995. WordNet: A Lexical Database for English. Communications of the ACM, 38(11):39–41.

Finn Årup Nielsen. 2018. Linking ImageNet WordNet Synsets with Wikidata. In WWW '18 Companion: The 2018 Web Conference Companion, pages 1809–1814, Lyon, France.

Princeton University. 2010. About WordNet. Princeton University, Princeton, NJ 08544, USA.

Yasser Regragui, Lahsen Abouenour, Fettoum Krieche, Karim Bouzoubaa, and Paolo Rosso. 2016. Arabic WordNet: New content and new applications Arabic WordNet. In Proceedings of the Eighth Global WordNet Conference, number January, pages 330–338.

Stephen Roller and Sabine Schulte. 2013. A Multimodal LDA Model Integrating Textual, Cognitive and Visual Modalities. In Proceedings of the 2013 Conference on Empirical Methods in Natural Language Processing, number October, pages 1146–1157, Seattle,Washington, USA. Association for Computational Linguistics.

Olga Russakovsky, Jia Deng, Hao Su, Jonathan Krause, Sanjeev Satheesh, Sean Ma, Zhiheng Huang, Andrej Karpathy, Aditya Khosla, Michael Bernstein, Alexander C Berg, and Li Fei-fei. 2015. ImageNet large scale visual recognition challenge. International Journal of Computer Vision, 115(3):211–252.

Shreya Shankar, Yoni Halpern, Eric Breck, James Atwood, Jimbo Wilson, and D Sculley. 2017. No Classification without Representation: Assessing Geodiversity Issues in Open Data Sets for the Developing World. In NIPS 2017 workshop: Machine Learning for the Developing World.

Ftoon Abu Shaqra, Rehab Duwairi, and Mahmoud Al-ayyoub. 2019. The Audio-Visual Arabic Dataset for Natural Emotions. In 2019 7th International Conference on Future Internet of Things and Cloud (FiCloud) The. IEEE.

Pierre Stock and Moustapha Cisse. 2018. ConvNets and ImageNet Beyond Accuracy: Understanding Mistakes and Uncovering Biases. In ECCV (6), pages 504–519.

Alakananda Vempala and Daniel Preot. 2019. Categorizing and Inferring the Relationship between the Text and Image of Twitter Posts. In Proceedings of the 57th Annual Meeting of the Association for Computational Linguistics, pages 2830–2840, Florence, Italy, July 28 - August 2, 2019. Association for Computational Linguistics.

Kaiyu Yang, Klint Qinami, Li Fei-Fei, Jia Deng, and Olga Russakovsky. 2020. Towards Fairer Datasets: Filtering and Balancing the Distribution of the People Subtree in the ImageNet Hierarchy. In Conference on Fairness, Accountability, and Transparency (FAT* '20), pages 547–558, Barcelona, Spain. ACM.

Mingyang Zhou, Runxiang Cheng, Yong Jae Lee, and Zhou Yu. 2018. A Visual Attention Grounding Neural Model for Multimodal Machine Translation. In Proceedings of the 2018 Conference on Empirical Methods in Natural Language Processing, pages 3643–3653, Brussels, Belgium, October 31 - November 4, 2018. Association for Computational Linguistics.

Toward General Scene Graph: Integration of Visual Semantic Knowledge with Entity Synset Alignment

Woo Suk Choi
Seoul National University
wschoi@bi.snu.ac.kr

Kyoung-Woon On
Seoul National University
kwon@bi.snu.ac.kr

Yu-Jung Heo
Seoul National University
yjheo@bi.snu.ac.kr

Byoung-Tak Zhang
Seoul National University
AI Institute (AIIS)
btzhang@bi.snu.ac.kr

Abstract

Scene graph is a graph representation that explicitly represents high-level semantic knowledge of an image such as objects, attributes of objects and relationships between objects. Various tasks have been proposed for the scene graph, but the problem is that they have a limited vocabulary and biased information due to their own hypothesis. Therefore, results of each task are not generalizable and difficult to be applied to other down-stream tasks. In this paper, we propose Entity Synset Alignment(ESA), which is a method to create a general scene graph by aligning various semantic knowledge efficiently to solve this bias problem. The ESA uses a large-scale lexical database, WordNet and Intersection of Union (IoU) to align the object labels in multiple scene graphs/semantic knowledge. In experiment, the integrated scene graph is applied to the image-caption retrieval task as a down-stream task. We confirm that integrating multiple scene graphs helps to get better representations of images.

1 Introduction

Beyond detecting and recognizing individual objects, research for understanding visual scenes is moving toward extracting semantic knowledge to create scene graph from natural images. Starting with (Krishna et al., 2017), various studies have been proposed to generate this semantic knowledge from images (Zellers et al., 2018; Xu et al., 2017; Liang et al., 2019; Anderson et al., 2018). However, each study extracts only highly biased information from an image due to the limited vocabulary depending on their own hypothesis and the statistical bias of the dataset. For example, in (Anderson et al., 2018), the author conducted a study on extracting information of both object and attribute for each entity using 1,600 object and 400 attribute class labels. In addition, (Zellers et al., 2018; Xu et al., 2017) generate a relationship between objects in a form of triplet *(head entity - predicate - tail entity)* in an image by using 150 object and 50 predicate class labels. In (Liang et al., 2019), the author constructed a Visually-Relevant Relationships(VrR-VG) based on (Krishna et al., 2017) to mine more valuable relationships with 1600 objects and 117 predicate class labels. As such, each task defines and uses its own vocabulary, but the problem is that the vocabulary is limited. As shown in Figure 1,If some of objects in an image do not belong to the dataset-specific vocabulary, objects as well as relations are omitted frequently even though they are in an image. In addition, there are cases where the same object is defined with different vocabulary in a common image (e.g. man, person).

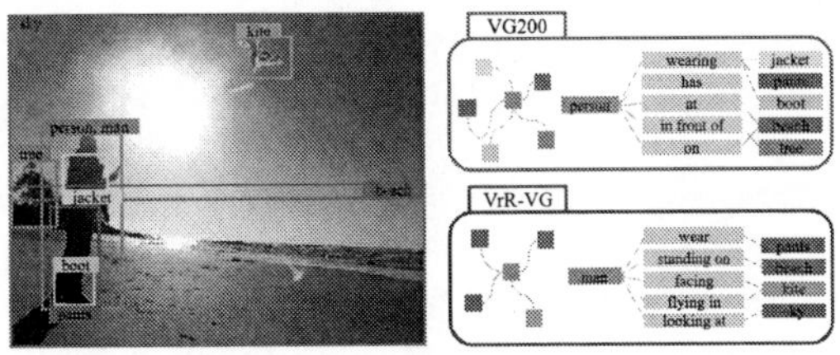

Figure 1: An example of scene graph for a common image from Visual Genome 200 (VG200) and Visually-Relevant Relationship (VrR-VG) dataset.

In this paper, we propose Entity Synset Alignment (ESA) to perform scene graph integration. With a large-scale lexical database WordNet and IoU, the ESA aligns the entity labels in scene graphs generated from each dataset. The contributions of the method proposed in this paper are as follows: 1) Scene graphs can be generated from raw image inputs, 2) integrating multiple scene graphs inferred from each dataset into one via ESA, 3) the qualitative results show that an integrated scene

Proceedings of the First Workshop on Advances in Language and Vision Research, pages 7–11

graph can extract richer semantic information in an image, 4) quantitative results show the significance of integrated scene graph by applying integrated scene graph to image-caption retrieval task.

2 Related Work

BottomUp-VG. Bottom-Up VG is a bottom-up attention model that extracts information of both object and attribute for each entity with 1,600 object and 400 attribute class labels from Visual Genome(VG).

VG200. VG200 introduced by (Xu et al., 2017) is a filtered version of the original VG scene graph dataset. It contains 150 object and 50 predicate class labels in 108,077 images, and consists of an average of 11.5 distinct objects and 6.2 predicates per image.

VrR-VG. Visually-Relevant Relationships (VrR-VG) introduced by (Liang et al., 2019) is constructed to highlight visually-relevant relationships using visual discriminator to learn the notion of visually-relevant.

WordNet. WordNet, a large lexical database of English, is an ontology that summarizes a relationship between words and has been integrated into the Natural Language ToolKit. Nouns, verbs, adjectives and adverbs are grouped into sets of cognitive synonyms (synsets), each representing intrinsic concept.

3 Method

As shown in Figure 2, we employ bottom-up attention (Anderson et al., 2018) model to generate only nodes containing information of both object and attribute, and CompTransR model to generate scene graphs from raw images. Entity Synset Alignment(ESA) integrates scene graphs generated from each dataset. We introduce a simple model, CompTransR, for scene graph generation in Section 3.1 and a scene graph integration technique, Entity Synset Alignment(ESA) in Section 3.2.

3.1 Compositional Translational Embedding

Compositional Translation Embedding combines the well-known Knowledge Graph embedding algorithms (i.e., TransR (Lin et al., 2015)) to learn the semantic relationships between two entities in a scene graph. Here, we apply transitive constraints to predict the semantic predicate labels in multiple symbolic subspaces by learning compositional representations of the relationships. As an entity feature, we extract visual, positional, and categorical features from a detected bounding box in a given image, and concatenate them into one. Then, entity features are transformed to head($\boldsymbol{h}$) and tail($\boldsymbol{t}$) features through single feed-forward neural network. The feature vectors of head and tail are projected into multiple latent relational subspaces. We aim to disentangle the semantic space of the sub-relation labels. The predicate representation $\boldsymbol{r}^s \approx \boldsymbol{t}^s - \boldsymbol{h}^s$ is defined on each latent relational space s. All $\boldsymbol{r}^s$ on the subspaces are summed out to predict predicate labels between two entities.

3.2 Entity Synset Alignment (ESA)

Algorithm 1: Entity Synset Alignment

```
Function ESA (A_obj_list, B_obj_list)
  obj_list=A_obj_list
for A_obj in A_obj_list do
    A_obj_synset = get_synset(A_obj);
    for B_obj in B_obj_list do
        B_obj_synset = get_synset(B_obj);
        if A_obj in B_obj_synset OR B_obj in
         A_obj_synset then
            iou = get_IoU(B_obj, A_obj);
            if iou is larger than 0.3 then
                pass_Flag=True;
                Break;
            end
        end
    end
    if pass_Flag is True then
        Continue;
    end
    obj_list.append(B_obj);
end
```

Entity Synset Alignment is an algorithm that integrates scene graphs generated from each dataset by using label alignment and Intersection of Union (IoU). In label alignment process, we use a synset, a set of synonym(lemma, hypernym, and hyponym) that shares a common meaning in WordNet, to align two entity labels. The method using synset compares whether an entity label in a scene graph is the same entity label in other scene graph, and aligns. If the entity label is same vocabulary or in the synset of entity label for other scene graph, then IoU calculation is implemented to check whether it indicates same entity. The detailed procedure is shown in Algorithm 1.

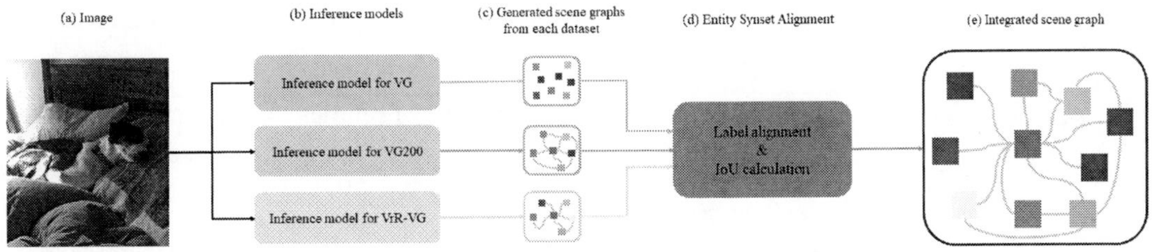

Figure 2: An overview of framework which integrates visual semantic knowledge with Entity Synset Alignment(ESA). (a) A raw image goes into inference models as an input. (b) Inference models(Bottom-up attention and CompTransR) generate (c) scene graphs from each dataset(VG, VG200, VrR-VG). (e) Integrated scene graph is built as an output via (d) Entity Synset Alignment method.

4 Experiments

4.1 Scene Graph Statistics

In Table 1, we measure the average and max number of object, relation, and attribute with various combinations of scene graph datasets. Default VG200 has 12.53 average number of object and 62 max number of object, default BottomUp-VG has 26.35 average number of object and 55 for max, and default VrR-VG has 36.77 average number of object and 167 max number of object. The most key section of Table 1 is the average number of object and relation in integrating three datasets increased. This result implies that integrating three scene graphs into one scene graph can get more richer scene graph.

4.2 Image-Caption Retrieval Task

To verify the usefulness of our algorithm, we suggest an image-caption retrieval task (Kiros et al., 2014) as an application of scene graphs. The image-caption retrieval task needs visual-semantic embeddings, which is obtained by mapping the image features and caption features into joint embedding space. A general approach for this task is to obtain image features and caption features with pre-trained model (such as VGGNet (Simonyan and Zisserman, 2014) for images and S-BERT (Reimers and Gurevych, 2019) for captions), then to learn mapping both to joint embedding space for maximizing similarities. In our case, we substitute image features from the pre-trained CNN model to scene-graphs and learn the representations of scene-graphs with simple 2-layer Graph Convolution Networks (Kipf and Welling, 2016). Following (Faghri et al., 2017), we use the *Max of Hinge* loss for training:

$$l_{MH}(i,c) = \max_{c'}[\alpha + s(i,c') - (i,c)]_+ + \max_{i'}[\alpha + s(i',c) - (i,c)]_+ \quad (1)$$

where i and c are image features and caption features in joint embedding space, $s(x,y)$ is inner-product similarity function for x and y, $[x] \equiv max(x,0)$ and α serves as a margin parameter.

4.3 Results

4.3.1 Qualitative Results

Figure 3 shows each generated scene graph for an image and an integrated scene graph generated. In each scene graph, person is presented as *person* in BottomUp-VG, but *woman* in VG200 and VrR-VG. Furthermore, *phone* and *tree(s)* nodes are in BottomUp-VG and VrR-VG, but not in VG200. On the other hand, BottomUp-VG and VrR-VG have *grass* node but not in VG200. In integrated scene graph, each node has an attribute of each object such as color and some entities such as person or tree are aligned via ESA. For the setting of qualitative results, we limit the number of relation(predicate) between objects to top 20 in generated each scene graph.

4.3.2 Quantitative Results

To obtain both captions and scene-graphs for images, we select subset of images, called VG-COCO, belongs to both MS COCO dataset (Lin et al., 2014) (for captions) and Visual Genome (VG) dataset (Krishna et al., 2017) (for scene graphs). We manually split the VG-COCO dataset with 24,763 train, 1,000 validation and 1,470 test images. To evaluate the performance of image-caption retrieval task, we introduce $Recall@K(R@K)$, i.e., the fraction of

Table 1: The average and max number of object, relation and attribute with various combinations of scene graph datasets.

Method	Number of object		Number of relation		Number of attributes	
	Avg.	Max	Avg.	Max	Avg.	Max
VG200	12.53	62	50.0	50	0.0	0
VrR-VG	36.77	167	50.0	50	0.0	0
BU-VG	26.35	55	0.0	0	26.35	55
VG200 $\wedge$ VrR-VG	37.00	167	100	100.0	0.0	0
VG200 $\wedge$ BU-VG	27.21	66	44.39	50	26.35	55
VrR-VG $\wedge$ BU-VG	42.04	141	29.57	50	26.35	55
VG200 $\wedge$ VrR-VG $\wedge$ BU-VG	41.95	127	79.67	100	26.35	55

Table 2: Quantitative results for our method on image-to-caption retrieval(caption retrieval) and caption-to-image retrieval(image retrieval) task. BU-VG is an abbreviation of BottomUp-VG.

	Method	Caption Retrieval			Image Retrieval		
		R@1	R@5	R@10	R@1	R@5	R@10
CNN based	ResNet-152	26.9	65.1	79.4	24.2	36.4	39.9
GCN based	VG200	22.2	57.6	73.2	19.7	34.6	39.5
	VrR-VG	28.1	66.2	80.4	23.2	37.2	40.9
	BU-VG	27.0	65.4	80.6	23.1	37.0	40.7
	VG200 $\wedge$ VrR-VG	29.3	67.6	81.9	23.4	37.4	41.0
	VG200 $\wedge$ BU-VG	29.4	68.7	82.8	24.1	37.5	41.1
	VrR-VG $\wedge$ BU-VG	27.9	70.5	83.2	23.7	37.7	41.4
	VG200 $\wedge$ VrR-VG $\wedge$ BU-VG	27.2	70.0	82.4	24.7	37.7	41.0

queries for which the correct item is retrieved in the closest K points to the query in the embedding space. We adopt R@1, R@5, R@10 metrics, as used in (Faghri et al., 2017).

First, to understand the effectiveness of scene graph based approach, we compare graph based method (GCN based) to CNN based model (Resnet-152). ResNet-152 trains the whole CNN networks, starting from pretrained model parameters. Here, we note that graph based method shows superior performance than the CNN based model, even though the graph based model exploits the simple two-layer graph convolution operations.

Second, we evaluate our proposed method with various combinations of VG200, VrR-VG and BottomUp-VG. The results show that integrated scene graph generally works better than default scene graph. The overall quantitative results for image-caption retrieval are presented in Table 2.

5 Conclusion

In this paper, we present a simple and efficient method to integrate multiple visual semantic knowledge into general scene graph. With a large-scale lexical database WordNet and IoU, the ESA aligns the entity labels in scene graphs generated from each dataset. The integrated scene graph has richer information and is less biased. To evaluate our proposal, we conduct the image-caption retrieval task as a down-stream task and show better performance than each scene graph. For future work, we plan to integrate more diverse visual semantic knowledge such as Human-object interaction (Gkioxari et al., 2018).

Acknowledgments

This work was partly supported by the Institute for Information and Communications Technology Promotion (2015-0-00310-SW.StarLab, 2017-0-01772-VTT, 2018-0-00622-RMI, 2019-0-01367-BabyMind) and Korea Institute for Advancement Technology (P0006720-GENKO) grant funded by the Korea government.

References

Peter Anderson, Xiaodong He, Chris Buehler, Damien Teney, Mark Johnson, Stephen Gould, and Lei Zhang. 2018. Bottom-up and top-down attention for

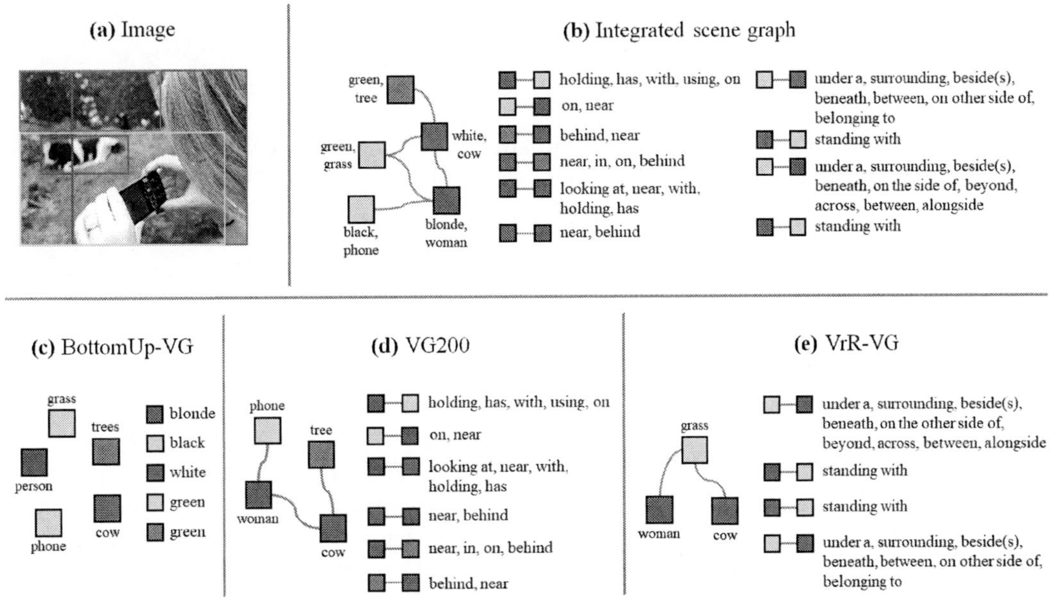

Figure 3: Qualitative results for our Entity Synset Alignment(ESA) method with Top 20 relations. Each scene graph (c),(d),(e) generated from inference models are combined into an integrated scene graph (b) for an image (a).

image captioning and visual question answering. In *CVPR*.

Fartash Faghri, David J Fleet, Jamie Ryan Kiros, and Sanja Fidler. 2017. Vse++: Improving visual-semantic embeddings with hard negatives. *arXiv preprint arXiv:1707.05612*.

Georgia Gkioxari, Ross Girshick, Piotr Dollár, and Kaiming He. 2018. Detecting and recognizing human-object interactions. In *Proceedings of the IEEE Conference on Computer Vision and Pattern Recognition*, pages 8359–8367.

Thomas N Kipf and Max Welling. 2016. Semi-supervised classification with graph convolutional networks. *arXiv preprint arXiv:1609.02907*.

Ryan Kiros, Ruslan Salakhutdinov, and Richard S Zemel. 2014. Unifying visual-semantic embeddings with multimodal neural language models. *arXiv preprint arXiv:1411.2539*.

Ranjay Krishna, Yuke Zhu, Oliver Groth, Justin Johnson, Kenji Hata, Joshua Kravitz, Stephanie Chen, Yannis Kalantidis, Li-Jia Li, David A Shamma, et al. 2017. Visual genome: Connecting language and vision using crowdsourced dense image annotations. *International Journal of Computer Vision*, 123(1):32–73.

Yuanzhi Liang, Yalong Bai, Wei Zhang, Xueming Qian, Li Zhu, and Tao Mei. 2019. Vrr-vg: Refocusing visually-relevant relationships. In *Proceedings of the IEEE International Conference on Computer Vision*, pages 10403–10412.

Tsung-Yi Lin, Michael Maire, Serge Belongie, James Hays, Pietro Perona, Deva Ramanan, Piotr Dollár, and C Lawrence Zitnick. 2014. Microsoft coco: Common objects in context. In *European conference on computer vision*, pages 740–755. Springer.

Yankai Lin, Zhiyuan Liu, Maosong Sun, Yang Liu, and Xuan Zhu. 2015. Learning entity and relation embeddings for knowledge graph completion. In *Twenty-ninth AAAI conference on artificial intelligence*.

Nils Reimers and Iryna Gurevych. 2019. Sentence-bert: Sentence embeddings using siamese bert-networks. *arXiv preprint arXiv:1908.10084*.

Karen Simonyan and Andrew Zisserman. 2014. Very deep convolutional networks for large-scale image recognition. *arXiv preprint arXiv:1409.1556*.

Danfei Xu, Yuke Zhu, Christopher B Choy, and Li Fei-Fei. 2017. Scene graph generation by iterative message passing. In *Proceedings of the IEEE Conference on Computer Vision and Pattern Recognition*, pages 5410–5419.

Rowan Zellers, Mark Yatskar, Sam Thomson, and Yejin Choi. 2018. Neural motifs: Scene graph parsing with global context. In *Proceedings of the IEEE Conference on Computer Vision and Pattern Recognition*, pages 5831–5840.

Visual Question Generation from Radiology Images

Mourad Sarrouti **Asma Ben Abacha** **Dina Demner-Fushmen**
National Library of Medicine, National Institutes of Health
Bethesda, MD
{mourad.sarrouti, asma.benabacha}@nih.gov, ddemner@mail.nih.gov

Abstract

Visual Question Generation (VQG), the task of generating a question based on image contents, is an increasingly important area that combines natural language processing and computer vision. Although there are some recent works that have attempted to generate questions from images in the open domain, the task of VQG in the medical domain has not been explored so far. In this paper, we introduce an approach to generation of visual questions about radiology images called VQGR, i.e. an algorithm that is able to ask a question when shown an image. VQGR first generates new training data from the existing examples, based on contextual word embeddings and image augmentation techniques. It then uses the variational auto-encoders model to encode images into a latent space and decode natural language questions. Experimental automatic evaluations performed on the VQA-RAD dataset of clinical visual questions show that VQGR achieves good performances compared with the baseline system. The source code is available at https://github.com/sarrouti/vqgr.

1 Introduction

VQG refers to generating natural language questions based on the images contents. It is a new and exciting problem that combines both natural language processing (Sarrouti and Alaoui, 2017, 2020) and computer vision techniques (Mostafazadeh et al., 2016; Zhang et al., 2016). The motivation for the VQG task is two-fold: (1) generating large scale Visual Question Answering (VQA) pairs to produce more training data at little cost (Ben Abacha et al., 2019) and (2) improving efficiency of human annotation for VQA datasets construction (Li et al., 2018). In addition to the aforementioned motivations, medical VQG could also benefit both doctors and patients. For example, patients could use questions provided by VQG systems to better understand medical images and start a conversation with their doctors. Moreover, such systems could support medical education, medical decision, and patient education (Lau et al., 2018).

A few recent works have attempted to generate questions from images in the open domain. However, the task of VQG in the medical domain has not been studied or explored. One major problem with medical VQG is the lack of large scale labeled training data which usually requires huge efforts to build.

In this paper, we introduce VQGR, a VQG system that is able to generate natural language questions when shown radiology images. In summary, this paper makes the following contributions:

1. To the best of our knowledge, generating questions based on images contents has not been explored in the medical domain. This work is the first attempt to generate questions about radiology images.
2. In the medical domain, the lack of large sets of labeled data makes training supervised learning approaches inefficient. To overcome the data limitation of medical VQG, we present data augmentation on both the images and the questions.
3. VQGR is based on the variational auto-encoders architecture and designed so that it can take a radiology image as input and generate a natural question as output.
4. Experimental evaluations performed on the VQA-RAD dataset of clinical questions and radiology images show that VQGR is effective.

Proceedings of the First Workshop on Advances in Language and Vision Research, pages 12–18

The paper is organized as follows: Section 2 surveys related work. Section 3 describes the proposed VQG approach. Section 4 presents experimental results and discussion.

2 Related Work

Question generation, an increasingly important area, is the task of automatically creating natural language questions from a range of inputs, such as natural language text (Kalady et al., 2010; Kim et al., 2019; Li et al., 2019), structured data (Serban et al., 2016) and images (Mostafazadeh et al., 2016). In this work, we are interested in generating questions from medical images. VQG in the open-domain benefited from the available large annotated datasets (Agrawal et al., 2015; Goyal et al., 2019; Johnson et al., 2017). There is a variety of work studying generative models for generating visual questions in the open domain (Masuda-Mora et al., 2016; Zhang et al., 2016). Recent VQG approaches have used autoencoders architecture for the purposes of VQG (Jain et al., 2017; Li et al., 2018; Krishna et al., 2019). The successes of these systems have primarily been a result of variational autoencoders (VAEs) (Kingma and Welling, 2013). Conversely, VQG in the medical domain is still a challenging and under-explored task (Hasan et al., 2018; Ben Abacha et al., 2018, 2019).

Although a high-quality manually created medical VQA dataset exists, VQA-RAD (Lau et al., 2018), this dataset is too small for training and there is a need for VQG approaches to create training datasets of sufficient size. Generating new training data from the existing examples through data augmentation is an effective approach that has been widely used to handle the data insufficiency problem in the open domain (Şahin and Steedman, 2018; Kobayashi, 2018). Due to the problem of data scarcity in medical VQG, we automatically generate new training data. In this paper, we present VQGR, a VQG system capable of generating questions about radiology images. The system is based on the VAE architecture and data augmentation.

3 Methods

The goal of this study is to generate natural language questions based on radiology image contents. The overview of VQGR is shown in Figure 1.

3.1 Data Augmentation

Questions. We generated new training examples based on question augmentation. For a given medical question q, we generate a set of new questions. During the augmenting process, we use all the VQA-RAD training data $D = \{q_i\}_{i=1}^{n}$ where n is the number of training questions. We expand each training question q_i into a set of instances q_i^k where k is the number of derived pairs for each training question. To do so, we first select nouns and verbs as candidate words, using the part-of-speech tags *NN, NNS, NNPS, NNP, VBD, VBP, VBN, VBG, VBZ, VB*[1]. Each candidate word is then replaced by contextually similar words using Wiki-PubMed-PMC embedding[2] which was trained using four million English Wikipedia, PubMed, and PMC articles. Similar words k for a given word are retrieved from the word embeddings space using cosine similarity. We compute cosine similarity between a weight vector of the given word w_i in the question and the vectors for each word w_j in the pre-trained word embeddings. We carried out several experiments with $k = \{5, 10, 15, 20, 30\}$ and found that the best result in terms of evaluations metrics (described in Subsection 4.2) can be achieved with $k = 20$. For instance, for a given question "Are the kidneys normal?", we generate the followings questions: "Were the kidneys normal?", "Are the pancreas normal?, "Are the intestines normal?", "Are the isografted normal?", Are the livers normal?, "Are the lungs normal?", "Are the organs normal?", etc.

Images. We also generated new training instances based on image augmentation techniques. To do so, we applied flipping, rotation, shifting, and blurring techniques to all VQA-RAD training images.

3.2 Visual Question Generation

The proposed VQGR system is based on the variational autoencoders architecture (Kingma and Welling, 2013). It first encodes the image before generating the question. VAEs consist of two neural network modules, encoder, and decoder, for learning the probability distributions of data $p(x)$. The encoder creates a latent variable z from raw data x and transforms it into latent space $z - space$. The decoder plays the role of recovering x using z extracted from the latent space. Let $q(z|x)$

[1]We used NLTK to perform part-of-speech tagging.

[2]http://evexdb.org/pmresources/vec-space-models/

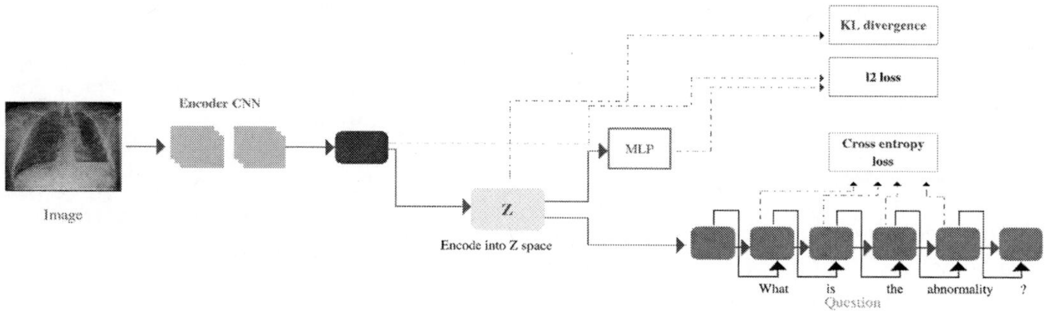

Figure 1: Overview of VQGR: a VQG model from radiology images.

and $p(x|z)$ be the probability distributions of the encoder and the decoder, respectively. Training of the encoder and decoder proceeds by maximizing marginal likelihood $\log p(x)$. Expanding the equation and finding the evidence lower bound (ELBO) yields:

$$\begin{aligned}\log p(x) \geq E_{z \sim q_\theta(z|x)}[\log p_\phi(x|z)] - \\ KL(q_\theta(z|x)||p(z)) \\ = ELBO\end{aligned} \tag{1}$$

The loss function of VAEs is the negative log-likelihood with a regularizer. The loss function l_i for datapoint x_i is:

$$\begin{aligned}l_i(\phi, \theta) = -E_{z \sim q_\theta(z|x_i)}[\log p_\phi(x_i|z)] + \\ KL(q_\theta(z|x_i)||p(z))\end{aligned} \tag{2}$$

where $E_{z \sim q_\theta(z|x_i)}[\log p_\phi(x_i|z)]$ is the reconstruction error and $KL(q_\theta(z|x)||p(z))$ is the Kullback-Leibler divergence regularization term. ϕ and θ, the parameters for the decoder distribution $p_\phi(x|z)$ and the encoder distribution $q_\theta(z|x)$ respectively.

Given an image v, a CNN is used for obtaining a feature map and encoding the dense vectors h_v into a latent (hidden) representation z-space. It then reconstructs the inputs from the z-space using a simple Multi Layer Perceptron (MLP) which is a neural network with fully connected layers. It generates the reconstructed image features $\hat{h_v}$ and optimizes the model by minimizing the following l_2 loss:

$$L_v = ||h_v - \hat{h_v}||_2 \tag{3}$$

We used the reparameterization trick (Kingma and Welling, 2013), to generate means μ_z and standard deviations σ_z, combine it with a sampled unit Gaussian noise ϵ to generate:

$$z = \mu_z + \epsilon\sigma_z \tag{4}$$

We assumed that z follows a multivariate Gaussian distribution with diagonal covariance.

Finally, it uses a decoder LSTM to generate the question $\hat{q}$ from the z-space. The decoder takes a sample from the latent dimension z-space, and uses that as an input to output the question $\hat{q}$. It receives a "start" symbol and proceeds to output a question word by word until it produces an "end" symbol. We used the Cross Entropy loss function to evaluate the quality of the neural network and to minimize the error L_g between the generated question $\hat{q}$ and the ground truth question q. The generation of each word of the question can be written:

$$\hat{w_t} = \arg\max_{w \in \mathbb{W}} p(w|v, w_0, ..., w_{t-1}) \tag{5}$$

where $\hat{w_t}$ is the predicted word at t step, $\mathbb{W}$ denotes the word vocabulary, and $\hat{w_i}$ represents the i-th ground-truth word.

The final loss of VQGR is as follows:

$$L_{VQGR} = \lambda_1 L_g + \lambda_2 KL + \lambda_3 L_v \tag{6}$$

where KL is Kullback-Leibler divergence which allows to know how well our variational posterior $q(z|v)$ approximates the true posterior $p(z|v)$. $\lambda_1, \lambda_2, \lambda_3$ are hyperparameters that control the variational loss, the question generation loss, and the reconstruction loss, respectively.

4 Experimental Results

4.1 Dataset

In this study, we used the VQA-RAD dataset (Lau et al., 2018) of clinical visual questions and images. It contains 315 images and 3,515 corresponding questions. Each image is associated with more than one questions. In this work, we are particularly interested in questions about 'Modality", "Abnormality", "Organ", and "Plane".

The training set consists of 69,598 questions and 1,673 images after applying data augmentation, and 1,269 questions and 239 images before data augmentation. Table 1 presents the number of questions and images associated to each of the selected categories. The test set contains 100 reference questions with associated categories and images.

Category	#Questions	#Images
Abnormality	397/18642	112/784
Modality	288/5534	54/378
Organ	73/16408	135/945
Plane	163/9216	99/693
Other	348/19798	81/567
Total	1269/69598	239/1673

Table 1: The number of questions and images associated to each category. The values after "/" represent the number of questions and images obtained by data augmentation techniques.

4.2 Evaluation Metrics

To investigate the performance of the proposed VQGR system, we perform both automatic and manual evaluations.

4.2.1 Automatic evaluation

VQG is a sequence generation problem. Therefore, we used a variety of language modeling evaluation metrics such as BLEU, ROUGE, METEOR, and CIDEr to measure the similarity between the system-generated questions and the ground-truth questions of the test set. We use the evaluation package published by (Chen et al., 2015).

4.2.2 Human evaluation

For human evaluation, we follow the standard approach in evaluating text generation systems (Koehn and Monz, 2006), as used for question generation by (Du and Cardie, 2018; Hosking and Riedel, 2019). We manually checked the generated questions and rated them in terms of relevancy, grammaticality, and fluency. The relevancy of a question is determined by the relationship between the question, image and category. Grammaticality refers to the conformity of a question to the grammar rules. Fluency refers to the way individual words sound together within a question. The rating process has been done by two experts at the U.S. National Institutes of Health. For each rating scheme, the human raters are required to give a rating ranging from 1 to 3 scale (1 = completely not satisfying the rating, 3 = fully satisfying the rating scheme).

4.3 Implementation Details

We implemented the VQGR and the baseline models using PyTorch. We used ImageNet-pretrained ResNet-50 (He et al., 2016) provided by PyTorch as the image encoder and do not fine-tune its weights. LSTM decoder is used for generating questions. All images are resized to 224*224. Adam optimiser with a learning rate of 0.0001 and a batch size of 32 is used. All models are trained for 40 epochs and the best validation results are used as final results. The source code is publicly available at `https://github.com/sarrouti/vqgr`.

4.4 Results and Discussion

Table 2 presents a comparison between the VQGR and the baseline systems in terms of multiple language modeling metrics. The baseline system is trained on the original VQA-RAD dataset without data augmentation. VQGR is trained on the data generated by our data augmentation techniques. We can see that VQGR performs significantly better across all metrics in comparison to the baseline model. The results demonstrate that our data augmentation techniques helped considerably, producing a significant improvement. As we discussed above, one major challenge in medical VQG is the lack of large training datasets. To avoid overfitting the model, small data might require models that have low complexity. Whereas the proposed VAE requires a large amount of training data as it tries to learn deeply the underlying data distribution of the input to output new sequences.

Model	B1	B2	B3	B4	M	RL	C
Baseline	31.4	14.6	7.8	3.2	10.4	38.8	21.1
VQGR	55.0	43.3	37.9	34.5	29.3	56.3	31.1

Table 2: Automatic evaluation results of the VQGR and the baseline models in terms of BLEU-1 (B1), BLEU-2 (B2), BLEU-3 (B3), BLEU-4 (B4), METEOR (M), ROUGE-L (RL) and CIDEr (C).

Table 3 shows the results of the human evaluation. We randomly selected 20 (image, question) pairs from the test set for a manual evaluation by two experts. Detailed guidelines for the raters are listed in subsection 4.2.2. Inter-rater reliability was calculated on each of the 3 measures.

F1-score for each measure is presented in Table 4. Most of the reliability scores are close to 0.50, which is considered satisfactory reliable. The human evaluation showed that VQGR achieves close to human performance in terms of relevancy, grammaticality, and fluency. We have not reported the human evaluation results of the baseline system since it returns the same trivial question "what is the abnormality in this image?" for all given images. This question could be asked about any radiology image, even a normal image, without even looking at it. Our goal is to develop approaches capable of asking non-trivial questions, which is not possible without understanding the image contents, at least to some extent.

Model	R	G	F	Score
VQGR	78.3	93.3	80.0	83.8

Table 3: Human evaluation results in terms of relevancy (R), grammaticality (G) and fluency (F). The score is the average of R, G and F. These numbers are the average of annotators scores and divided by 60 to have them between 0 and 1. The perfect score is 100.

Model	R	G	F
VQGR	0.42	0.27	0.51

Table 4: Inter-rater Reliability based on F1-score (Hripcsak, 2005). R, G and F indicate relevancy, grammaticality and fluency, respectively.

Overall, VQG in the medical domain is a very challenging task, and VQGR provides a practical alternative to generate visual questions about radiology images. Figure 2 provides example questions generated by Lau et al. (2018) (ground truth questions) and the VQGR system. From these samples, we can see that the generated questions are consistent with the ground truth.

5 Conclusion and Future Work

We presented the first attempt to generate visual questions in the medical domain. We first presented a data augmentation method to generate new training questions and images from the VQA-RAD dataset. We then introduced the VQGR model that generates questions from radiology images. The results of the automatic and manual evaluations showed that VQGR outperforms the baseline model by generating fluent and relevant questions.

In the future, we will investigate the use of the generated questions to advance VQA in the medical domain.

Image	Generated questions vs. ground truth
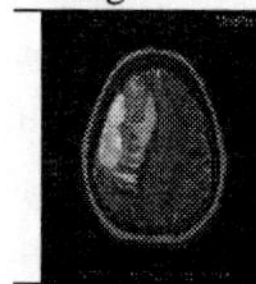	what type of mri is used to acquire this image ? mri imaging modality used for this image?
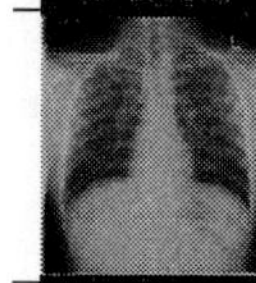	what is seen in the lung apices ? what abnormalities are in the lung apices ?
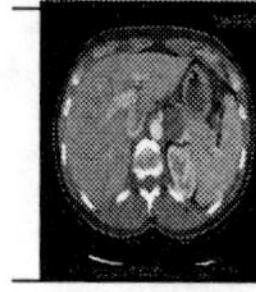	is a ring enhancing lesion present in the right lobe of the liver? is the liver normal ?

Figure 2: Examples of test images with the generated questions (shown in blue) and the ground truth.

Acknowledgements

This work was supported by the intramural research program at the U.S. National Library of Medicine, National Institutes of Health.

References

Aishwarya Agrawal, Jiasen Lu, Stanislaw Antol, Margaret Mitchell, C. Lawrence Zitnick, Dhruv Batra, and Devi Parikh. 2015. VQA: Visual Question Answering. In *2015 IEEE International Conference on Computer Vision (ICCV)*, pages 2425–2433.

Asma Ben Abacha, Soumya Gayen, Jason J. Lau, Sivaramakrishnan Rajaraman, and Dina Demner-Fushman. 2018. NLM at imageclef 2018 visual question answering in the medical domain. In *Working Notes of CLEF 2018 - Conference and Labs of the Evaluation Forum, Avignon, France, September 10-14, 2018*, volume 2125 of *CEUR Workshop Proceedings*. CEUR-WS.org.

Asma Ben Abacha, Sadid A. Hasan, Vivek V. Datla, Joey Liu, Dina Demner-Fushman, and Henning Müller. 2019. Vqa-med: Overview of the medical visual question answering task at imageclef 2019. In *Working Notes of CLEF 2019 - Conference and Labs of the Evaluation Forum, Lugano, Switzerland, September 9-12, 2019*, volume 2380 of *CEUR Workshop Proceedings*. CEUR-WS.org.

Xinlei Chen, Hao Fang, Tsung-Yi Lin, Ramakrishna Vedantam, Saurabh Gupta, Piotr Dollár, and C. Lawrence Zitnick. 2015. Microsoft COCO captions: Data collection and evaluation server. *ArXiv*, abs/1504.00325.

Xinya Du and Claire Cardie. 2018. Harvesting paragraph-level question-answer pairs from Wikipedia. In *Proceedings of the 56th Annual Meeting of the Association for Computational Linguistics (Volume 1: Long Papers)*, pages 1907–1917, Melbourne, Australia. Association for Computational Linguistics.

Yash Goyal, Tejas Khot, Aishwarya Agrawal, Douglas Summers-Stay, Dhruv Batra, and Devi Parikh. 2019. Making the V in VQA Matter: Elevating the Role of Image Understanding in Visual Question Answering. *Int. J. Comput. Vision*, 127(4):398–414.

Sadid A. Hasan, Yuan Ling, Oladimeji Farri, Joey Liu, Henning Müller, and Matthew P. Lungren. 2018. Overview of imageclef 2018 medical domain visual question answering task. In *Working Notes of CLEF 2018 - Conference and Labs of the Evaluation Forum, Avignon, France, September 10-14, 2018*, volume 2125 of *CEUR Workshop Proceedings*. CEUR-WS.org.

Kaiming He, Xiangyu Zhang, Shaoqing Ren, and Jian Sun. 2016. Deep Residual Learning for Image Recognition. In *2016 IEEE Conference on Computer Vision and Pattern Recognition (CVPR)*, pages 770–778.

Tom Hosking and Sebastian Riedel. 2019. Evaluating rewards for question generation models. In *Proceedings of the 2019 Conference of the North*. Association for Computational Linguistics.

G. Hripcsak. 2005. Agreement, the f-measure, and reliability in information retrieval. *Journal of the American Medical Informatics Association*, 12(3):296–298.

Unnat Jain, Ziyu Zhang, and Alexander Schwing. 2017. Creativity: Generating diverse questions using variational autoencoders. In *Proceedings - 30th IEEE Conference on Computer Vision and Pattern Recognition, CVPR 2017*, pages 5415–5424, United States. Institute of Electrical and Electronics Engineers Inc.

Justin Johnson, Bharath Hariharan, Laurens van der Maaten, Li Fei-Fei, C. Lawrence Zitnick, and Ross Girshick. 2017. Clevr: A diagnostic dataset for compositional language and elementary visual reasoning. In *2017 IEEE Conference on Computer Vision and Pattern Recognition (CVPR)*, pages 1988–1997.

Saidalavi Kalady, Ajeesh Elikkottil, and Rajarshi Das. 2010. Natural language question generation using syntax and keywords. In *Proceedings of QG2010: The Third Workshop on Question Generation*, volume 2, pages 5–14.

Yanghoon Kim, Hwanhee Lee, Joongbo Shin, and Kyomin Jung. 2019. Improving neural question generation using answer separation. In *Proceedings of the AAAI Conference on Artificial Intelligence*, volume 33, pages 6602–6609.

Diederik P Kingma and Max Welling. 2013. Auto-encoding variational bayes. *arXiv preprint arXiv:1312.6114*.

Sosuke Kobayashi. 2018. Contextual augmentation: Data augmentation by words with paradigmatic relations. In *Proceedings of the 2018 Conference of the North American Chapter of the Association for Computational Linguistics: Human Language Technologies, Volume 2 (Short Papers)*. Association for Computational Linguistics.

Philipp Koehn and Christof Monz. 2006. Manual and automatic evaluation of machine translation between european languages. In *Proceedings of the Workshop on Statistical Machine Translation - StatMT 06*. Association for Computational Linguistics.

Ranjay Krishna, Michael Bernstein, and Li Fei-Fei. 2019. Information maximizing visual question generation. In *Proceedings of the IEEE Conference on Computer Vision and Pattern Recognition*, pages 2008–2018.

Jason J. Lau, Soumya Gayen, Asma Ben Abacha, and Dina Demner-Fushman. 2018. A dataset of clinically generated visual questions and answers about radiology images. *Scientific Data*, 5(1).

Jingjing Li, Yifan Gao, Lidong Bing, Irwin King, and Michael R. Lyu. 2019. Improving question generation with to the point context. In *Proceedings of the 2019 Conference on Empirical Methods in Natural Language Processing and the 9th International Joint Conference on Natural Language Processing*, volume 33, page 3216–3226.

Yikang Li, Nan Duan, Bolei Zhou, Xiao Chu, Wanli Ouyang, and Xiaogang Wang. 2018. Visual Question Generation as Dual Task of Visual Question Answering. In *2018 IEEE/CVF Conference on Computer Vision and Pattern Recognition*, pages 6116–6124.

Issey Masuda-Mora, Santiago Pascual-deLaPuente, and Xavier Giró i Nieto. 2016. Towards automatic generation of question answer pairs from images. In *Visual Question Answering Challenge Workshop, CVPR 2016*, Las Vegas, NV, USA.

Nasrin Mostafazadeh, Ishan Misra, Jacob Devlin, Margaret Mitchell, Xiaodong He, and Lucy Vanderwende. 2016. Generating natural questions about an image. In *Proceedings of the 54th Annual Meeting of the Association for Computational Linguistics (Volume 1: Long Papers)*, pages 1802–1813, Berlin, Germany. Association for Computational Linguistics.

Gözde Gül Şahin and Mark Steedman. 2018. Data augmentation via dependency tree morphing for low-resource languages. In *Proceedings of the 2018 Conference on Empirical Methods in Natural Language Processing*. Association for Computational Linguistics.

Mourad Sarrouti and Said Ouatik El Alaoui. 2017. A passage retrieval method based on probabilistic information retrieval model and UMLS concepts in biomedical question answering. *Journal of Biomedical Informatics*, 68:96–103.

Mourad Sarrouti and Said Ouatik El Alaoui. 2020. Sembionlqa: A semantic biomedical question answering system for retrieving exact and ideal answers to natural language questions. *Artificial Intelligence in Medicine*, 102:101767.

Iulian Vlad Serban, Alberto García-Durán, Caglar Gulcehre, Sungjin Ahn, Sarath Chandar, Aaron Courville, and Yoshua Bengio. 2016. Generating factoid questions with recurrent neural networks: The 30m factoid question-answer corpus. In *Proceedings of the 54th Annual Meeting of the Association for Computational Linguistics*, page 588–598, Berlin, Germany. Association for Computational Linguistics.

Shijie Zhang, Lizhen Qu, Shaodi You, Zhenglu Yang, and Jiawan Zhang. 2016. Automatic generation of grounded visual questions. In *Proceedings of the Twenty-Sixth International Joint Conference on Artificial Intelligence (IJCAI-17)*, pages 4235–4243.

On the role of effective and referring questions in GuessWhat?!

Mauricio Mazuecos (1), Alberto Testoni (2), Raffaella Bernardi (3) and Luciana Benotti (1)
(1) FAMAF, Universidad Nacional de Córdoba, CONICET, Argentina
(2) DISI, University of Trento, Italy
(3) DISI, CIMEC, University of Trento, Italy
mmazuecos@famaf.unc.edu.ar alberto.testoni@unitn.it
raffaella.bernardi@unitn.it luciana.benotti@unc.edu.ar

Abstract

Task success is the standard metric used to evaluate referential visual dialogue systems. In this paper we propose two new metrics that evaluate how each question contributes to the goal. First, we measure how *effective* each question is by evaluating whether the question discards objects that are not the referent. Second, we define *referring* questions as those that univocally identify one object in the image. We report the new metrics for human dialogues and for state of the art publicly available models on GuessWhat?!. Regarding our first metric, we find that successful dialogues do not have a higher percentage of effective questions for most models. With respect to the second metric, humans make questions at the end of the dialogue that are referring, confirming their guess before guessing. Human dialogues that use this strategy have a higher task success but models do not seem to learn it.

1 Introduction

GuessWhat?! (de Vries et al., 2017) is a cooperative two-player referential visual dialogue game. One player (the *Oracle*) is assigned a referent object in an image, the other player (the *Questioner*) has to guess the referent by asking yes/no questions.

Referential visual dialogue has a clear task success metric: whether the Questioner is able to correctly identify the referent at the end of the dialogue. The need of going beyond this metric to evaluate the quality of the dialogues has already been observed. So far attention has been put on the linguistic skills of the models (Shukla et al., 2019; Shekhar et al., 2019) and their dialogue strategies (Shekhar et al., 2018; Pang and Wang, 2020). But still the models are evaluated without considering how much each question contributes to the goal. We propose two new metrics for evaluating questions. First, a question is *effective* if it rules out at least one possible distractor (Krahmer and van Deemter, 2012). Second, a question is *referring* if it uniquely identifies one object in the image.

Figure 1 gives a game played by humans as an example. In the image there are 8 candidate objects: the referent object is the cow marked in green and the distractors are the other 6 cows and the wooden stick. The dialogue is highly effective: 80% of the questions eliminate at least one distractor. The figure shows for each question its answer, how many distractors (#D) are left after each answer and whether the question is effective or not effective. The last question is not effective but it is referring, it uniquely identifies the referent. Interestingly, question 2 is also referring but not with respect to the referent, so the dialogue needs to go on.

In the next section we review previous work. Then, we define the metrics formally and calculate them over the Guesswhat?! SOTA models. Finally, we argue that models, differently from humans, do not confirm their guess before guessing.

2 Previous work

Despite recent progress in the area of vision and language, recent work (Jain et al., 2019) in the navigation task (VLN) argues that current research leaves unclear how much of a role language plays in this task. They point out that dominant evaluation metrics have focused on goal completion rather than how each action contributes to the goal. Historically, the performance of VLN models has been evaluated with respect to the objective of reaching the goal location (Anderson et al., 2018). The nature of the path an agent takes, however, is of clear practical importance: it is undesirable for any robotic agent in the physical world to reach the destination by taking a lot of deviation or getting into dangerous zones. Jain et al. (2019) propose alternative metrics that evaluate the intermediate

Proceedings of the First Workshop on Advances in Language and Vision Research, pages 19–25

Human question	Answer	#D	Effective
1. is it a cow?	yes	6	True
2. is it the big cow in the middle?	no	5	True
3. a cow on the left?	no	3	True
4. in the front?	yes	0	True
5. first cow near us on the right?	yes	0	False

Figure 1: Human-human dialogue on the Guesswhat?! referential task extracted from (de Vries et al., 2017). The referent is highlighted in green. #D is the number of distractors remaining after the question is answered. Four out of five questions eliminate distractors and, hence, are effective according to our definition. The last question is referring with respect to the intended referent.

steps taken towards the goal for the VLN task.

As argued by (Lowe et al., 2019), the vast majority of recent papers on emergent communication show that adding a communication channel leads to an increase in task success. This is a useful indicator, but provides only a coarse measure of the agent's learned communication abilities. As we move towards more complex environments, it becomes imperative to have a set of finer tools that allow qualitative and quantitative insights into the emergence of communication. This may be especially useful to allow humans to monitor agents' behaviour, whether for fault detection, assessing performance, or even building trust.

Following this idea of not only focusing on goal completion but on evaluating how much each step contributes to the goal, in this paper we propose two new metrics for referential dialogue. We agree with (Thomason et al., 2019) that incremental evaluation metrics such as ours should look further back into the dialogue history. We believe that language and vision systems should also be evaluated on aspects such as grammatically, truthfulness, diversity and other aspects as done in previous work (Lee et al., 2018; Ray et al., 2019; Xie et al., 2020; Murahari et al., 2019). In this paper we focus on whether a question is effective and referential considering the dialogue history and the visual context.

One of the motivations for referential visual dialogue is to provide robots with the ability to identify objects through dialogue with a human as the robot moves. The task we address in this paper is a simplification. In our setup, the view of the robot is static, it is a picture. For our work we use the GuessWhat?! dataset (de Vries et al., 2017).

Recently, Sankar et al. (2019) showed that several end-to-end dialogue systems do not take dialogue history into account. In this paper we are particularly interested in the GuessWhat?! models that generate questions explicitly modelling the dialogue history (Zhang et al., 2018; Shukla et al., 2019; Pang and Wang, 2020).[1]

3 Dataset and Evaluation Metrics

In this section we briefly introduce the dataset and we define the evaluation metrics that we use.

3.1 GuessWhat?!

GuessWhat?! (de Vries et al., 2017) is a cooperative game where two players talk in order to identify an object in an image. The player known as the *Questioner* has to guess the referent by asking yes/no questions. The other player, the *Oracle*, knows the referent object and answers the questions. The GuessWhat?! dataset contains games of different complexity, ranging from easy images with the referent and only one distractor, to images with up to 19 distractors. The dataset is composed of more than 150k human-human dialogues containing an average of 5.3 questions in natural language created by turkers playing the game on MS COCO images (Lin et al., 2014).

3.2 Effective and referring questions

Our definition of *effective question* is based on the set of candidate objects: the *reference set* RS. We compute RS for each question q_t. The reference set before the dialogue starts, $RS(q_0)$, contains all the objects in the image. That is, it contains the list of objects annotated in the dataset and given to the Oracle model. Human Oracles did not have access to this list. At each dialogue turn t, $RS(q_t)$ is the set of objects in $RS(q_{t-1})$ such that the answer A to q_t on those objects is the same than the answer to q_t on the referent r. All answers A are computed using the Oracle proposed in (de Vries et al., 2017)

[1] Unfortunately, the code or test dialogues of some previous work are not available (Zhang et al., 2018; Shukla et al., 2019).

whose accuracy on the test set is 79%. Formally:

$$RS(q_t) := \{o_i \in RS(q_{t-1}) \mid A(q_t, o_i) = A(q_t, r)\}$$

We say that a question q_t is *not effective* iff $RS(q_t) = RS(q_{t-1})$; that is, the question does *not* exclude any distractor. In our definition, an *effective* question excludes at least one distractor; hence, $RS(q_t) \subset RS(q_{t-1})$. The effectiveness of the dialogue is given by the percentage of effective questions it has. In the example given in Figure 1, the last question of the dialogue, namely, *"first cow near us on the right?"* is not effective by our definition. Strictly speaking, it does not exclude any distractor and the human could have guessed after turn 4. This last question verifies the guessed referent by constructing a referring expression for it that is relative to the speaker's position. We say that this question is *referring*.

We say that a question q_t is *referring* wrt the referent r iff $A(q_t, r) =$ *"yes"* and $A(q_t, o_i) =$ *"no"* for all other objects o_i in the image. As we do with effectiveness, we calculate A by using the Oracle model (de Vries et al., 2017) repeateadly over all objects. That is, if a question uniquely identifies the referent then its answer is "yes" only for the referent. In the example in Figure 1, the last question is not effective but it is referring, it uniquely identifies the referent. Interestingly, question 2 is also referring but not with respect to the referent, so the dialogue needs to go on. One may expect that referring questions are realized using the definite determiner "the" as in question 2, but this is not always the case as observed in question 5.

4 Experiments and results

In this section we describe the GuessWhat!? SOTA models for which the code or the test set dialogues have been released and we present our results.

4.1 Models and experiments

Models usually implement the Questioner player using two agents: the QGen which generates the questions and the Guesser which takes a finished dialogue and makes a guess for the referent.

We took the dialogues generated by different SOTA models on the test set of the split defined in (de Vries et al., 2017). The Baseline (BL) model proposed by de Vries et al. (2017) is an encoder-decoder architecture conditioned by image and dialogue features for the QGen. Its Guesser is a MLP that embeds the list of candidate objects and chooses the referent conditioned by the dialogue and the image features. The Reinforcement Learning (RL) model (Strub et al., 2017) casts the problem into a reinforcement learning task and trains the previous model with policy gradient. The Visually-Grounded State Encoder (GDSE) models, both Supervised Learning (SL) and Cooperative Learning (CL) (Shekhar et al., 2019) use a visually grounded dialogue state that takes the visual features and each new question to create a shared representation used for both QGen and Guesser. They differ in that SL is trained in a supervised fashion while CL samples new objects from pictures and makes the agents train in a cooperative learning fashion on those artificially generated games. Last, Visual Dialogue State Tracking (VDST) (Pang and Wang, 2020) extends the QGen with a representation of the probability of each object being the referent.

For each of the models, we calculate the reference sets for each question in their dialogues. We calculated the percentage of effective questions in each dialogue comparing failed and successful dialogues. For the last question in each dialogue we calculate whether it is effective and/or referring.

4.2 Results

In this section we first exemplify our metrics over dialogues generated by two models and then present the quantitative results.

Figure 2 shows an example of both metrics on a game on which VDST and CL are successful. Effectiveness is 60 for VDST and 40 for CL. Our definition of effectiveness not only accounts for question repetitions, but it also captures paraphrases and context-dependent redundancies. Examples of context dependent redundancy can be seen for both systems. In the VDST dialogue, 4 is redundant because, in this image, there is no cake that is both in the front and in the top. In CL dialogue, question 2 is redundant because all cakes in the image are dark brown. There are no referring questions in the VDST dialogue. The CL dialogue finishes with a referring and effective question that is realized using a definite article. The question even includes the connector "so" giving the feeling that the system intends to verify its guess. However, the same system uses a definite determiner in question 3 as if the question was referring but it is not (there are three dark brown cakes).

We report quantitative results for humans and

VDST		**GDSE-CL**	
1. is it food?	yes	1. is it food?	yes
2. is it in the left?	yes	2. *is it a cake?*	yes
3. is it in the front?	yes	3. *is it the dark brown?*	yes
4. *is it in the top?*	no	4. *is it the entire cake?*	yes
5. *in the middle?*	no	5. so the most left of the brown ones?	yes

Figure 2: Dialogues generated by VDST and CL in a successful game. Non effective in italics. There are no referring questions in the VDST dialogue. The CL dialogue finishes with a referring and effective question that is realized using a definite article.

for the 5-question and 8-question setups for SOTA models. Table 1 shows average number of questions (#Q), task success (TS) and effectiveness for each of the models and the human dialogues. The table also shows the percentage of dialogues whose last turn is effective and/or referring.

The results suggest that models make more non-effective questions than one may expect. Surprisingly, successful dialogues generated by models do not have a higher percentage of effective questions. Even for humans, effectiveness is not considerably higher for successful dialogues. Human effectiveness is higher in almost every column of the table, the VDST model is close. Humans do not see the list of annotated objects as the Guesser models do. They rely on their sight on the image and they may ask questions that discard objects present in the image but not annotated in the dataset and hence not part of the reference set we calculate. All of these questions are marked as non-effective because they discard objects invisible to our metric and to the models. Hence, human effectiveness could be higher than we have calculated using the GuessWhat?! dataset object annotations.

Humans and models alike ask non-effective questions mostly at the end of the dialogue. The effectiveness decreases as dialogue progresses for models and humans and reaches its lowest level in the last turn as shown in Table 1. Interestingly, models and humans seem to be using the last turn for different purposes. 26% of human dialogues end with a referring question while the model that reaches the highest value for this metric has only a 7%. We found that human task success for the dialogues that end with a referring question is 95% while it is 80% for the rest.

4.3 Analysis of Oracle accuracy

The computation of both metrics involves using an automatic Oracle. Even though this Oracle achieves high accuracy on the test set, this accuracy is actually measured on human-generated questions. In this section we evaluate this Oracle calculating its accuracy for different types of questions. We also report the different types of questions that the systems produce. The types of questions generated by systems show a distribution shift from those generated by humans. We argue that machine-generated questions are easier and the performance of the Oracle should be equal or higher for them than for the human ones.

Following Shekhar et al. (2019), we classify questions into different types and evaluate the Oracle accuracy for each type. We distinguish between eight types of questions. The first type are those that include a noun representing the category of the referent (e.g., 'is it a dog?'); we use the categories of objects defined in MS COCO (Lin et al., 2014). Then we consider questions about properties usually realized as adjectives or prepositional phrases. We make a distinction between color, shape, size, texture, location, and action questions. The classification is done by extracting keywords for each question type from the human dialogues, and then assigning each question to as many types as it fits. A question may be tagged with several attribute classes if more than one keyword is present. E.g., "Is it the white one on the left?" is classified as both color and location. The list of keywords is available in (Shekhar et al., 2019).

In Table 2 we can see that the distribution of types of questions varies from model to model and differs to the distribution in humans. Humans make more questions about the color, size, shape of the target as well as about the action that the target is performing (e.g. "is she skiing?"). Some models make more questions about the object (e.g. BL, SL and CL) and about the location (e.g. RL and VDST). The table also reports the Oracle accuracy on the human dataset per type of question. The

Model	#Q	TS	Effectiveness			Last Turn	
			All	Failure	Success	Effective	Referring
BL (de Vries et al., 2017)	8	40.7	26.4	27.5	24.7	4.2	4.46
SL (Shekhar et al., 2019)	8	49.7	29.1	31.4	26.9	7.4	5.64
RL (Strub et al., 2017)	8	56.3	32.6	36.5	29.6	3.5	2.60
CL (Shekhar et al., 2019)	8	58.4	30.2	32.3	28.6	7.6	6.08
BL (de Vries et al., 2017)	5	40.8	38.8	39.8	37.4	11.9	5.20
SL (Shekhar et al., 2019)	5	47.8	42.2	44.6	39.9	16.4	7.42
RL (Strub et al., 2017)	5	58.4	48.6	52.9	45.1	23.0	2.68
CL (Shekhar et al., 2019)	5	53.7	44.7	47.8	42.6	18.5	6.32
VDST (Pang and Wang, 2020)	5	64.4	52.9	57.4	51.0	28.7	1.82
Humans (H) (de Vries et al., 2017)	5.3	84.1	56.9	54.7	57.3	33.6	26.01

Table 1: Task success (TS), Effectiveness and Last Turn Effectiveness by model in the test set. Effectiveness is reported for all dialogues and dialogues ending in failure or success. For VDST we only report the results for 5 question dialogues as we only had access to these dialogues. For the last turn of the dialogues we report the percentage of effective and referring questions.

hardest types of question for the Oracle are color and size questions. All models ask fewer of these questions than humans. Also most models, except for VDST and RL, ask more object questions than humans; this is the type of question for which the Oracle has the highest accuracy. The models VDST and RL ask more location questions. However, we have manually observed that the location questions that cause more errors for the Oracle are questions regarding order (e.g. "the third counting from the left?"). Such questions constitute 8% of the human questions and have an accuracy of 58% but are not made by VDST and RL. The type of location questions asked by VDST are illustrated in Figure 2. We have argued that models make questions that are easier for the Oracle than those made by humans. We hypothesize that the Oracle accuracy is then higher for machine-generated questions. We will investigate this hypothesis further in future work.

Type	Acc	BL	SL	RL	CL	VDST	H
Obj	94	49.00	48.08	24.00	46.40	36.44	38.12
Color	63	2.75	13.00	0.12	12.51	0.01	15.50
Shape	67	0.00	0.01	0.00	0.02	0.00	0.30
Size	60	0.02	0.33	0.02	0.39	0.01	1.38
Tex	70	0.00	0.33	0.01	0.15	0.00	0.89
Loc	67	47.25	37.09	74.80	38.54	64.80	40.00
Act	65	1.34	7.97	0.66	7.60	0.30	7.59
Other	75	1.12	5.28	0.49	5.90	0.03	8.60

Table 2: Oracle accuracy per type of question and question distribution for the models. We report BL, SL, RL and CL question type distribution with 8 questions, and VSDT with 5 questions and the human dialogues.

5 Conclusions

We proposed two new metrics for evaluating Guesswhat?! dialogues. Effectiveness, as we defined it, evaluates whether the question can rule out at least one possible distractor. We consider a question to be effective if it is able to make the reference set smaller both if the question is answered with 'yes' as well as if it is answered with 'no'. We observe that it decreases as dialogues advance and reaches its lowest level in the last turn. We also find that successful dialogues do not have a higher percentage of effective questions. This is surprising, and hints at the fact that there are other strategies to accomplish reference identification other than asking effective questions. One of such strategies is captured by our second metric: questions that may not be effective but are referring.

Humans seem to use the last turn to confirm their guess before guessing. Human dialogues that confirm the guess using a referring questions have a higher task success than those which do not. We plan to explore whether models can learn to confirm their guess before guessing. As future work we plan to refine our referring metric. We have observed that some dialogues do not make explicit the object category in the confirmation. E.g. "the one near us on the right?" in Figure 1. By our definition, this question would not be referring because it is also true for the wooden stick.

We believe that our metrics could be heuristics that guide the training of end-to-end models.

References

Peter Anderson, Angel X. Chang, Devendra Singh Chaplot, Alexey Dosovitskiy, Saurabh Gupta, Vladlen Koltun, Jana Kosecka, Jitendra Malik, Roozbeh Mottaghi, Manolis Savva, and Amir Roshan Zamir. 2018. On evaluation of embodied navigation agents. *CoRR*, abs/1807.06757.

Vihan Jain, Gabriel Magalhaes, Alexander Ku, Ashish Vaswani, Eugene Ie, and Jason Baldridge. 2019. Stay on the path: Instruction fidelity in vision-and-language navigation. In *Proceedings of the 57th Annual Meeting of the Association for Computational Linguistics*, pages 1862–1872, Florence, Italy. Association for Computational Linguistics.

Emiel Krahmer and Kees van Deemter. 2012. Computational generation of referring expressions: A survey. *Computational Linguistics*, 38(1):173–218.

Sang-Woo Lee, Yu-Jung Heo, and Byoung-Tak Zhang. 2018. Answerer in questioner's mind: Information theoretic approach to goal-oriented visual dialog. In S. Bengio, H. Wallach, H. Larochelle, K. Grauman, N. Cesa-Bianchi, and R. Garnett, editors, *Advances in Neural Information Processing Systems 31*, pages 2579–2589. Curran Associates, Inc.

Tsung-Yi Lin, Michael Maire, Serge Belongie, James Hays, Pietro Perona, Deva Ramanan, Piotr Dollár, and C. Lawrence Zitnick. 2014. Microsoft COCO: Common objects in context. In *Computer Vision - ECCV 2014 - 13th European Conference, Zurich, Switzerland, September 6-12, 2014, Proceedings, Part V*, pages 740–755, Cham. Springer.

Ryan Lowe, Jakob Foerster, Y-Lan Boureau, Joelle Pineau, and Yann Dauphin. 2019. On the pitfalls of measuring emergent communication. In *Proceedings of the 18th International Conference on Autonomous Agents and MultiAgent Systems*, AAMAS '19, page 693–701, Richland, SC. International Foundation for Autonomous Agents and Multiagent Systems.

Vishvak Murahari, Prithvijit Chattopadhyay, Dhruv Batra, Devi Parikh, and Abhishek Das. 2019. Improving generative visual dialog by answering diverse questions. In *Proceedings of the 2019 Conference on Empirical Methods in Natural Language Processing and the 9th International Joint Conference on Natural Language Processing (EMNLP-IJCNLP)*, pages 1449–1454, Hong Kong, China. Association for Computational Linguistics.

Wei Pang and Xiaojie Wang. 2020. Visual dialogue state tracking for question generation. In *Proceedings of the Thirty-Fourth AAAI Conference on Artificial Intelligence (AAAI)*.

Arijit Ray, Karan Sikka, Ajay Divakaran, Stefan Lee, and Giedrius Burachas. 2019. Sunny and dark outside?! improving answer consistency in VQA through entailed question generation. In *Proceedings of the 2019 Conference on Empirical Methods in Natural Language Processing and the 9th International Joint Conference on Natural Language Processing (EMNLP-IJCNLP)*, pages 5860–5865, Hong Kong, China. Association for Computational Linguistics.

Chinnadhurai Sankar, Sandeep Subramanian, Chris Pal, Sarath Chandar, and Yoshua Bengio. 2019. Do neural dialog systems use the conversation history effectively? an empirical study. In *Proceedings of the 57th Annual Meeting of the Association for Computational Linguistics*, pages 32–37, Florence, Italy. Association for Computational Linguistics.

Ravi Shekhar, Tim Baumgärtner, Aashish Venkatesh, Elia Bruni, Raffaella Bernardi, and Raquel Fernandez. 2018. Ask no more: Deciding when to guess in referential visual dialogue. In *Proceedings of the 27th International Conference on Computational Linguistics*, pages 1218–1233, Santa Fe, New Mexico, USA. Association for Computational Linguistics.

Ravi Shekhar, Aashish Venkatesh, Tim Baumgärtner, Elia Bruni, Barbara Plank, Raffaella Bernardi, and Raquel Fernández. 2019. Beyond task success: A closer look at jointly learning to see, ask, and GuessWhat. In *Proceedings of the 2019 Conference of the North American Chapter of the Association for Computational Linguistics: Human Language Technologies, Volume 1 (Long and Short Papers)*, pages 2578–2587, Minneapolis, Minnesota. Association for Computational Linguistics.

Pushkar Shukla, Carlos Elmadjian, Richika Sharan, Vivek Kulkarni, Matthew Turk, and William Yang Wang. 2019. What should I ask? using conversationally informative rewards for goal-oriented visual dialog. In *Proceedings of the 57th Annual Meeting of the Association for Computational Linguistics*, pages 6442–6451, Florence, Italy. Association for Computational Linguistics.

Florian Strub, Harm de Vries, Jeremie Mary, Bilal Piot, Aaron C. Courville, and Olivier Pietquin. 2017. End-to-end optimization of goal-driven and visually grounded dialogue systems. In *International Joint Conference on Artificial Intelligence (IJCAI)*.

Jesse Thomason, Michael Murray, Maya Cakmak, and Luke Zettlemoyer. 2019. Vision-and-dialog navigation. In *Conference on Robot Learning*, Osaka, Japan.

Harm de Vries, Florian Strub, Sarath Chandar, Olivier Pietquin, Hugo Larochelle, and Aaron C. Courville. 2017. Guesswhat?! visual object discovery through multi-modal dialogue. In *Conference on Computer Vision and Pattern Recognition (CVPR)*.

Huiyuan Xie, Tom Sherborne, Alexander Kuhnle, and Ann Copestake. 2020. Going beneath the surface: Evaluating image captioning for grammaticality, truthfulness and diversity. In *Workshop on Evaluating AI Systems (AAAI 2020)*.

Junjie Zhang, Qi Wu, Chunhua Shen, Jian Zhang, Jianfeng Lu, and Anton van den Hengel. 2018. Goal-oriented visual question generation via intermediate rewards. In *Computer Vision - ECCV 2018 - 15th European Conference, Munich, Germany, September 8-14, Proceedings, Part V*, volume 11209 of *Lecture Notes in Computer Science*, pages 189–204. Springer.

Latent Alignment of Procedural Concepts in Multimodal Recipes

Hossein Rajaby Faghihi, Roshanak Mirzaee, Sudarshan Paliwal and **Parisa Kordjamshidi**
Michigan State University
{rajabyfa, mirzaeem, paliwal, kordjams}@msu.edu

Abstract

We propose a novel alignment mechanism to deal with procedural reasoning on a newly released multimodal QA dataset, named RecipeQA. Our model is solving the textual cloze task which is a reading comprehension on a recipe containing images and instructions. We exploit the power of attention networks, cross-modal representations, and a latent alignment space between instructions and candidate answers to solve the problem. We introduce constrained max-pooling which refines the max-pooling operation on the alignment matrix to impose disjoint constraints among the outputs of the model. Our evaluation result indicates a 19% improvement over the baselines.

1 Introduction

Procedural reasoning by following several steps to achieve a goal is an essential part of our daily tasks. However, this is challenging for machines due to the complexity of instructions and commonsense reasoning required for understanding the procedure (Dalvi et al., 2018; Yagcioglu et al., 2018; Bosselut et al., 2017).

In this paper, we tackle the task of procedural reasoning in a multimodal setting for understanding cooking recipes. The RecipeQA dataset (Yagcioglu et al., 2018) contains recipes from internet users. Thus, understanding the text is challenging due to the different language usage and informal nature of user-generated texts. The recipes are along with images provided by users which are taken in an unconstrained environment. This exposes a level of difficulty similar to real-world problems.

The tasks proposed with the dataset include textual cloze, visual cloze, visual ordering, and visual coherence. Here, we focus on textual cloze. An example of this task is shown in Figure 1. The input to the task is a set of multimodal instructions, three textual items from the question and a placeholder to be filled by the answer. The answer has to be chosen from four options. The three question items and the correct answer make a sequence which correctly describes the steps of the recipe.

To design our model, we rely on the intuition that given question items, each answer describes exactly one step of the recipe. Hence, we design a model to make explicit alignments between the candidate answers and each step and use those alignment results, given the question information. This alignment space is latent due to not having any direct supervision based on provided annotations.

Using multimodal information and representations by making a joint space for comparison has been broadly investigated in the recent research (Hessel et al., 2019; Wu et al., 2019; Li et al., 2019; Su et al., 2020; Yu et al., 2019; Fan and Zhou, 2018; Tan and Bansal, 2019; Nam et al., 2017). Our work differs from those as we do not have direct supervision on multimodal alignments. Moreover, the task we are solving uses the sequential nature of visual and textual modality as a weak source of supervision to build a neural model to compare the textual representation of context and the answers for a given question representation.

Procedural reasoning has been investigated on different tasks (Amac et al., 2019; Park et al., 2017). While PRN (Amac et al., 2019) is proposed on RecipeQA, their model does not apply to the textual cloze task. (Park et al., 2017) is using procedural reasoning on multimodal information to generate a story from a sequence of images. However, the textual cloze task is about filling a blank in a sequence given a set of textual options.

Our model exploits the latent alignment space and the positional encoding of questions and answers while applying a novel approach for constraining the output space of the latent alignment. Moreover, we exploit cross-modality representa-

Proceedings of the First Workshop on Advances in Language and Vision Research, pages 26–31

Pizza Pancakes

Step1: You need the following ingredients ... 400 gr. flour 3 eggs ...
Step2: Take a bowl and add the flour and ...
Step3: Take a cutting board and knife ...
Step4: Bake the veggies in separate pieces...
Step5: Heat up the pan and poor a little ...

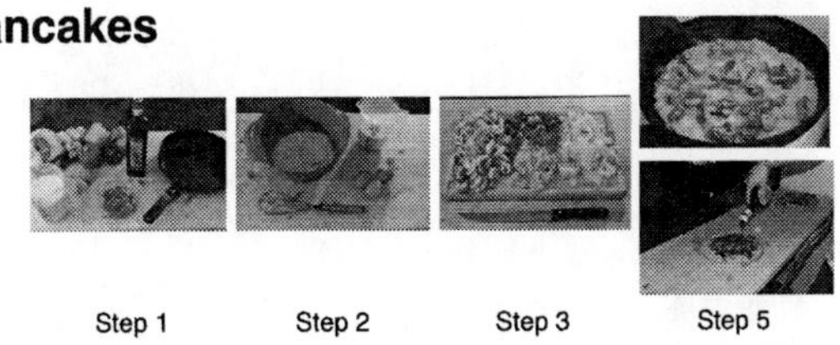

Question: Choose the best title for the missing blank to correctly complete the recipe.
________. Making the Dough. Preparing Veggies. Baking.

Answers: (A.) Preparation B. Pizza Cones C. Fillings D. Cut the Portrait

Figure 1: A sample of textual cloze task

tions based on cross attention to investigate the benefits from information flow between images and instructions. We compare our results to the provided baselines in (Yagcioglu et al., 2018) and achieve the state-of-the-art by improving over 19%.

2 Proposed Model

We design a model to solve a structured output prediction on the textual cloze task. The intuition of our model is that the correct answer option should describe precisely one instruction, and this instruction should not be already described with other items in the question. Hence, our model assumes the instruction and question as the context and candidate answers as an additional input to the alignment process. Moreover, to incorporate the order of the sequence in question items and the placeholder, we utilize a one-hot encoding vector of positions to be concatenated with the candidate answers and question items' representations.

We give the instructions to a sentence splitter using Stanford Core NLP library (Manning et al., 2014). The output is then tokenized by Flair data structure (Akbik et al., 2018) and embedded with BERT (Devlin et al., 2019). The words' embeddings are passed to an LSTM layer and the last layer is used as the instruction representation. We propose two different approaches to include images representations. These proposals are described in Section 3.3. An overview of our approach is shown in Figure 2.

Question representation is the last layer of an LSTM on question items. The representation of each question item is the concatenated vector of a one-hot position encoding and word embedding obtained from BERT. The candidate answers' representations are computed using the same approach. We concatenate the question representation to each instruction. Then, the similarity of each candidate answer and instruction is computed using the cosine similarity and form a similarity matrix. We use S to denote the similarity matrix. The rows of this matrix are candidate answers and the columns represent the recipe steps. The value of S_{ij} indicates the similarity score of candidate i and step j.

For training the model, we define two different objectives directly applied to the similarity matrix. The textual cloze task does not have the direct supervision required for the alignment between candidates and steps, and our objective is designed to use the answer of the question to train this latent space of alignments. For imposing the constraint of the alignment to be disjoint between steps and candidates, one way is to simply compute the maximum of each row in the similarity matrix and use that as the aligned step for each candidate answer; However, we introduce constrained max-pooling which is a more sophisticated approach as shown in Figure 3. We compare these two alternatives in the experimental results. We apply an iterative process to select the most related pair of instruction (a column) and answer candidate (a row) while removing the related column and row each time until all candidate answers find their aligned instruction. We denote the final selected maximum scores by $m = (S_{1i_1}, S_{2i_2}, S_{3i_3}, S_{4i_4})$, where $i_c \in [1, number\_of\_steps]$ is the index of the step with maximum alignment score with candidate $c$and for all pairs of candidates c and d, $c \neq d \implies i_c \neq i_d$.

Respectively, we define two following objectives. The first objective maximizes the distance between the maximum score of the correct answer and the

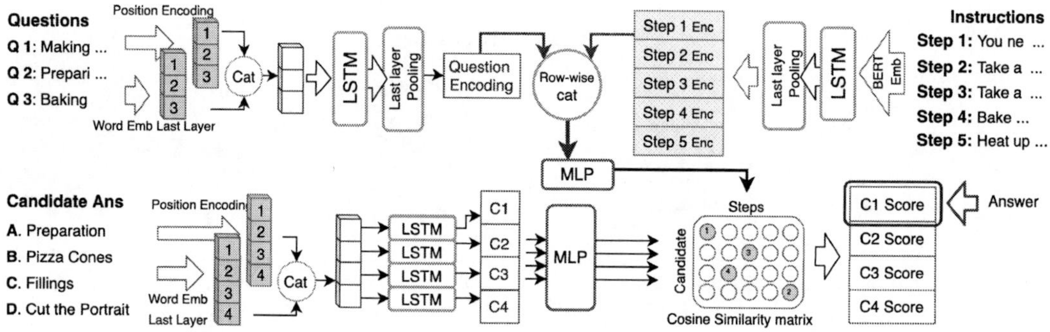

Figure 2: An overview of proposed model

maximum score of another random wrong answer candidate. Furthermore, by fixing the instruction with the maximum alignment with the correct answer, it decreases the score of the other candidates alignments with that instruction. The second objective, increases the maximum similarity score of the answer to approach to 1 while decreasing the other maximum scores to be lower than 0.1.

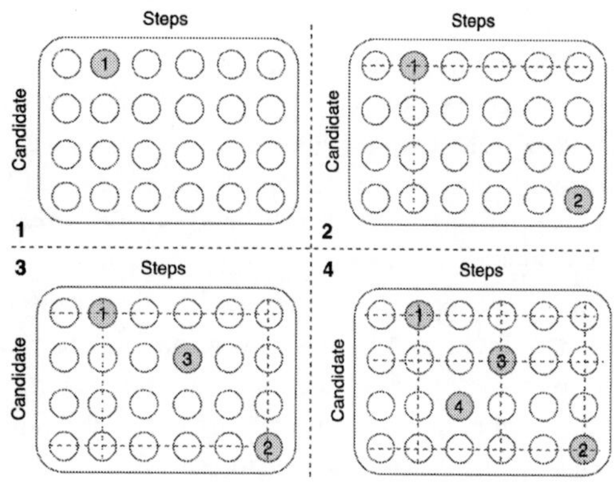

Figure 3: The matrix operation for constrained max-pooling

$$Loss = \max(0, S_{ri_r} - S_{ai_a} + 0.1) + \sum_{c \neq a}^{4} \max(0, S_{ci_a} - S_{ai_a} + 0.1) \quad (1)$$

$$Loss = (1 - S_{ai_a}) + \sum_{c \neq a}^{4} \max(0, S_{ci_c} - 0.1) \quad (2)$$

Where $a \in \{1, 2, 3, 4\}$ is the correct answer number and r is a random index from $\{1, 2, , 3, 4\} - \{a\}$. The main difference in objective 1 and objective 2 is the regularization term on the selected instruction column in the alignment matrix.

3 Experiment

3.1 Baselines

Hasty Student (Tapaswi et al., 2016) is a simple approach considering only the similarity between elements in question and candidate answers. This baseline fails to get good results due to the intrinsic of the task.

Impatient Reader (Hermann et al., 2015) computes attention from answers to the recipe for each candidate and despite being a complicated approach, yet it fails to get good results on the task. Moreover, multimodal Impatient reader approach uses both instructions and corresponding images.

3.2 Results

The RecipeQA textual cloze task contains 7837 training, 961 validation, and 963 test examples. A learning rate of $4 - e1$ is used for the first half and then $8 - e2$ for the second half of training iterations. We use the momentum of 0.9 for all variations of our model. We train for 30 iterations with a batch size of 1 and optimize the weights using an SGD optimizer. For word embedding, the pre-trained BERT embedding in Flair framework is used. For the image representations, ResNet50 (He et al., 2016) pre-trained on Imagenet (Russakovsky et al., 2015) using PyTorch library (Paszke et al., 2019) is applied.

Table 1 presents the experimental results. We call the model variations which use the loss objective in Equation (1) as Model-obj 1 and the ones that use the loss in Equation (2) as Model-obj 1. Using the objective in Formula (1) yields better results in all experiments. This indicates the benefit of using the column-wise disjoint constraint on the similarity matrix. Also, using multimodal information yields 1.12% improvement. We elaborate further on the comparison between multimodal and unimodal results in Section 4.

We provide our Pytorch implementation publicly available on Github [1].

3.3 Multimodal Results

In order to investigate the usefulness of the images in solving the textual cloze task, we propose two different models that incorporate the image representation in addition to the textual information of recipe steps. The first variation receives ResNet50 representations of the images and, after applying an LSTM layer, pulls the last layer as image representation. Finally, it concatenates the image representation to the question and instruction representation in the main architecture before applying the MLP and computing the cosine similarities.

The second variation as shown in figure 4, uses a more complex architecture introduced in LXMERT (Tan and Bansal, 2019). We modify the architecture of LXMERT and apply it to the word embedding and image representations to flow the information from each to another. The updated word embedding and image representations are passed to an LSTM, and its last layer is used to represent the visual and textual information of a step. In the end, these representations are concatenated to each other and the question representation to build the instruction vector representation. We report the results of these model variations in Table 1. Using the cross modality representations based on LXMERT provided extensive way to flow the information from text and image to each other and yields the best results.

4 Discussion and Analysis

We did qualitative analysis using some examples and their results to better understand the behaviour of the proposed model. Our model is almost able to detect all matched candidates with the instructions (in case that there exist multiple matches) but fails to choose the one that completes the sequence of the question items. This indicates the shortage of procedural hints inside our architecture while the latent alignment is proven to be practical. By analysing the results, we found interesting cases

[1] https://github.com/HLR/LatentAlignmentProcedural

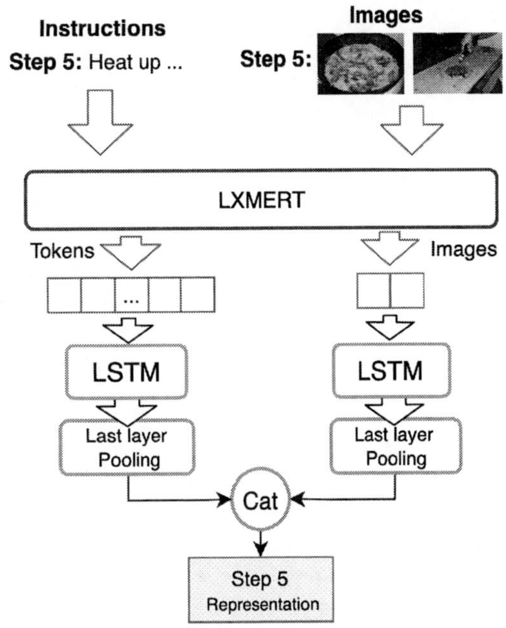

Figure 4: Using LXMERT for integrating multimodal information on steps

where either multimodal or unimodal architectures could yield more accurate predictions.

Multimodal - , Unimodal +:

- Images contain misleading information (see example in Figure 5).
- Image quality is low.
- Images are not showing the steps correctly.
- Text contains direct mentions of candidate answers.

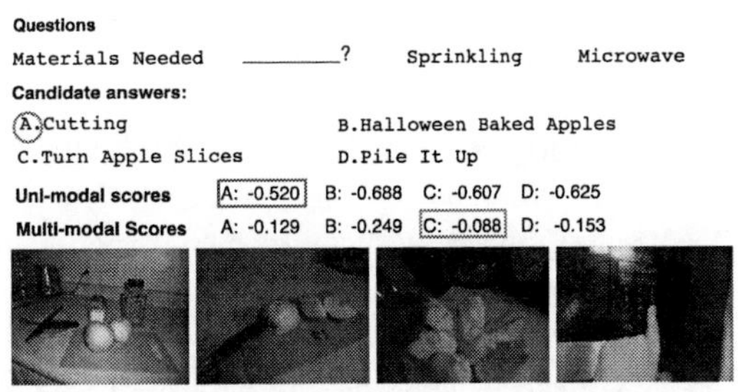

Figure 5: The image is misleading the multimodal setting to choose apple slices rather than cutting option

Multimodal + , Unimodal -:

- The sequence of the images provide detailed steps and good quality.
- The entities in candidates answers are shown in the pictures but not in the text.
- The recipes instructions are very short and the images provide more information.

Models	Accuracy	p@2
Human	73.6	-
Hasty Student	26.89	-
Impatient Reader	28.03	-
Impatient Reader (multimodal)	29.07	-
Model-Obj 1	46.35	**78.7**
Model-Obj 2	43.36	-
Model-Obj 1 (multimodal)	45.41	
Model-Obj 1 (multimodal) + LXMERT	**47.5**	77.5
Model-Obj 1 (multimodal) + LXMERT - ConstrainedMaxPooling	46.9	76.3

Table 1: Evaluation on the test set

In some cases, the multimodal information can fix the errors resulted from not considering the order of events in the proposed architecture. Our intuition is that, although, the textual model does not contain information from previous steps, the images carry useful information on what has been already done. An example of this is shown in Figure 6, where co-reference resolution is required to answer the question correctly.

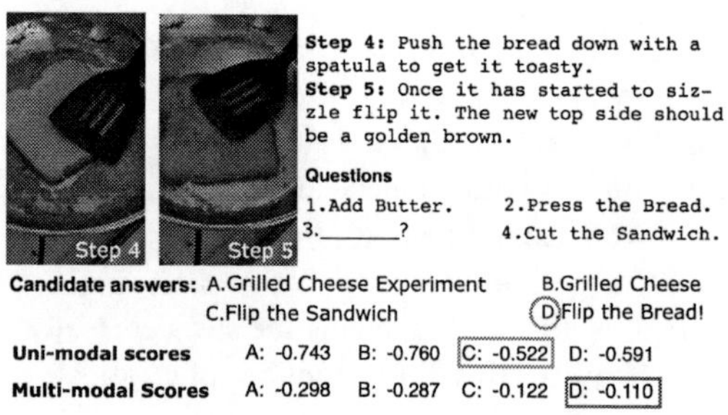

Figure 6: The images lead the model to understand that "it" refers to bread rather than sandwich

Furthermore, we have tested our multimodal architecture with representations of ResNet101 and the results dropped. We confirmed this experiment by re-implementing Hasty Student approach on visual coherence task (that has 68% accuracy with ResNet50) and obtained 35% lower than ResNet50. This can be due to the lack of quality of images resulting in extra noise when using a more complicated network. Thus, ResNet50 achieves better accuracy by producing more abstract representations of the images.

5 Conclusion and Future Work

We proposed a model for RecipeQA textual cloze task which exploits the latent alignment of question items with instructions. Moreover, we investigated the benefit of using multimodal information in this task by comparing three different architectures and provided qualitative analysis on some examples to justify the results. Our model exceeded the baselines and improved the SOTA by over 19%. As a future direction, we will investigate the usage of the latent alignment in other tasks. We will apply more complex methods on textual abstractions and attention mechanisms to link the candidate answers with the recipe instructions. Investigating how to incorporate the question order in the architecture is another direction.

Acknowledgments

This work is (partially) supported by the Office of Naval Research grant N00014-19-1-2308.

References

Alan Akbik, Duncan Blythe, and Roland Vollgraf. 2018. Contextual string embeddings for sequence labeling. In *COLING 2018, 27th International Conference on Computational Linguistics*, pages 1638–1649.

Mustafa Sercan Amac, Semih Yagcioglu, Aykut Erdem, and Erkut Erdem. 2019. Procedural reasoning networks for understanding multimodal procedures. In *Proceedings of the 23rd Conference on Computational Natural Language Learning (CoNLL)*, pages 441–451, Hong Kong, China. Association for Computational Linguistics.

Antoine Bosselut, Omer Levy, Ari Holtzman, Corin Ennis, Dieter Fox, and Yejin Choi. 2017. Simulating action dynamics with neural process networks. In *Sixth International Conference on Learning Representations (ICLR)*.

Bhavana Dalvi, Lifu Huang, Niket Tandon, Wen-tau Yih, and Peter Clark. 2018. Tracking state changes in procedural text: a challenge dataset and models for process paragraph comprehension. In *Proceedings of the 2018 Conference of the North American Chapter of the Association for Computational Linguistics: Human Language Technologies, Volume 1 (Long Papers)*, pages 1595–1604, New Orleans, Louisiana. Association for Computational Linguistics.

Jacob Devlin, Ming-Wei Chang, Kenton Lee, and Kristina Toutanova. 2019. BERT: Pre-training of deep bidirectional transformers for language understanding. In *Proceedings of the 2019 Conference of the North American Chapter of the Association for Computational Linguistics: Human Language Technologies, Volume 1 (Long and Short Papers)*, pages 4171–4186, Minneapolis, Minnesota. Association for Computational Linguistics.

Haoqi Fan and Jiatong Zhou. 2018. Stacked latent attention for multimodal reasoning. In *Proceedings of the IEEE Conference on Computer Vision and Pattern Recognition*, pages 1072–1080.

Kaiming He, Xiangyu Zhang, Shaoqing Ren, and Jian Sun. 2016. Deep residual learning for image recognition. In *Proceedings of the IEEE conference on computer vision and pattern recognition*, pages 770–778.

Karl Moritz Hermann, Tomas Kocisky, Edward Grefenstette, Lasse Espeholt, Will Kay, Mustafa Suleyman, and Phil Blunsom. 2015. Teaching machines to read and comprehend. In *Advances in neural information processing systems*, pages 1693–1701.

Jack Hessel, Lillian Lee, and David Mimno. 2019. Unsupervised discovery of multimodal links in multi-image, multi-sentence documents. In *EMNLP*.

Liunian Harold Li, Mark Yatskar, Da Yin, Cho-Jui Hsieh, and Kai-Wei Chang. 2019. Visualbert: A simple and performant baseline for vision and language. *arXiv preprint arXiv:1908.03557*.

Christopher D Manning, Mihai Surdeanu, John Bauer, Jenny Rose Finkel, Steven Bethard, and David McClosky. 2014. The stanford corenlp natural language processing toolkit. In *Proceedings of 52nd annual meeting of the association for computational linguistics: system demonstrations*, pages 55–60.

Hyeonseob Nam, Jung-Woo Ha, and Jeonghee Kim. 2017. Dual attention networks for multimodal reasoning and matching. In *Proceedings of the IEEE Conference on Computer Vision and Pattern Recognition*, pages 299–307.

Cesc Chunseong Park, Youngjin Kim, and Gunhee Kim. 2017. Retrieval of sentence sequences for an image stream via coherence recurrent convolutional networks. *IEEE transactions on pattern analysis and machine intelligence*, 40(4):945–957.

Adam Paszke, Sam Gross, Francisco Massa, Adam Lerer, James Bradbury, Gregory Chanan, Trevor Killeen, Zeming Lin, Natalia Gimelshein, Luca Antiga, Alban Desmaison, Andreas Kopf, Edward Yang, Zachary DeVito, Martin Raison, Alykhan Tejani, Sasank Chilamkurthy, Benoit Steiner, Lu Fang, Junjie Bai, and Soumith Chintala. 2019. Pytorch: An imperative style, high-performance deep learning library. In H. Wallach, H. Larochelle, A. Beygelzimer, F. dAlché-Buc, E. Fox, and R. Garnett, editors, *Advances in Neural Information Processing Systems 32*, pages 8024–8035. Curran Associates, Inc.

Olga Russakovsky, Jia Deng, Hao Su, Jonathan Krause, Sanjeev Satheesh, Sean Ma, Zhiheng Huang, Andrej Karpathy, Aditya Khosla, Michael Bernstein, et al. 2015. Imagenet large scale visual recognition challenge. *International journal of computer vision*, 115(3):211–252.

Weijie Su, Xizhou Zhu, Yue Cao, Bin Li, Lewei Lu, Furu Wei, and Jifeng Dai. 2020. Vl-bert: Pre-training of generic visual-linguistic representations. In *Eighth International Conference on Learning Representations (ICLR)*.

Hao Tan and Mohit Bansal. 2019. LXMERT: Learning cross-modality encoder representations from transformers. In *Proceedings of the 2019 Conference on Empirical Methods in Natural Language Processing and the 9th International Joint Conference on Natural Language Processing (EMNLP-IJCNLP)*, pages 5100–5111, Hong Kong, China. Association for Computational Linguistics.

Makarand Tapaswi, Yukun Zhu, Rainer Stiefelhagen, Antonio Torralba, Raquel Urtasun, and Sanja Fidler. 2016. Movieqa: Understanding stories in movies through question-answering. In *Proceedings of the IEEE conference on computer vision and pattern recognition*, pages 4631–4640.

Hao Wu, Jiayuan Mao, Yufeng Zhang, Yuning Jiang, Lei Li, Weiwei Sun, and Wei-Ying Ma. 2019. Unified visual-semantic embeddings: Bridging vision and language with structured meaning representations. In *Proceedings of the IEEE Conference on Computer Vision and Pattern Recognition*, pages 6609–6618.

Semih Yagcioglu, Aykut Erdem, Erkut Erdem, and Nazli Ikizler-Cinbis. 2018. RecipeQA: A challenge dataset for multimodal comprehension of cooking recipes. In *Proceedings of the 2018 Conference on Empirical Methods in Natural Language Processing*, pages 1358–1368, Brussels, Belgium. Association for Computational Linguistics.

Zhou Yu, Yuhao Cui, Jun Yu, Dacheng Tao, and Qi Tian. 2019. Multimodal unified attention networks for vision-and-language interactions. *arXiv preprint arXiv:1908.04107*.

Author Index

Association for Computational Linguistics
209 N. Eighth Street
Stroudsburg, Pennsylvania 18360

ISBN 978-1-7138-1375-0

CURRAN ASSOCIATES INC.
proceedings.com